D1412406

WITNESS TO JUSTICE

A SOCIETY TO BE TRANSFORMED

Working Instruments

Episcopal Commission For Social Affairs
Canadian Conference of Catholic Bishops

May, 1979

Approved by: Most Rev. John M. Sherlock, President, Social Life Department, Canadian Conference of Catholic Bishops; and Mgr Bernard Hubert, Chairman, Episcopal Commission for Social Affairs, Canadian Conference of Catholic Bishops.

The translation of the Medellin documents is taken from the "The Church in the Present-Day Transformation of Latin America in the Light of the Council, vol. 2, Conclusions", the official English edition published by the Latin American Bureau of the United States Catholic Conference and the General Secretariat of the Latin American Episcopal Council (CELAM). The Medellin Conference (Second General Conference of Latin American Bishops) took place August 24-September 6, 1968, in Bogota and Medellin, Columbia. The English translation appeared in 1970.

Witness to Justice: A Society to be Transformed, copyright ©Concacan Inc., 1979. All rights reserved. No part of this book may be reproduced in any form without permission in writing from the Social Affairs Desk.

If through inadvertence, anything has been printed without permission, proper acknowledgement will be made in future printings after notice has been received.

Published by: Publications Service
Canadian Conference of Catholic Bishops
90 Parent Avenue
OTTAWA, Ontario

Legal Deposit: National Library, Ottawa, Ontario, Canada

ISBN—English version: 0-88997-036-X
French version: 0-88997-038-6

Printed in Canada

Synopsis

PREFACE

In recent years, the demands for justice and liberation on the part of the poor, the oppressed, and the afflicted have been voiced with a new sense of urgency, at home and throughout the world. These demands have presented a major challenge to Christian communities and their ministry in proclaiming the Gospel message of love and justice for mankind in the world today.

The recent conference of bishops in Puebla, the visit of Pope Paul II to Latin America and Mexico, his encyclical **Redemptor Hominis,** provide vivid illustrations of the pastoral challenges facing the mission of the Church at this critical moment in history.

As the World Synod of Bishops stressed in 1971, participation in the struggles of justice and the transformation of society is not an optional activity for Christians. It is integral to the task of proclaiming the Gospel message of liberation and salvation. For God sent His Son to save mankind from the sins that separate man from God, including the social sins of injustice which cause poverty, hunger, misery, oppression, and exploitation.

Through recent social messages and pastoral action programmes, the Canadian bishops have urged Christians to follow Jesus Christ and proclaim His message: by modifying our more affluent life styles and opening our hearts to the poor in our midst; by listening and being present with the poor, the oppressed, and the afflicted; by analyzing the structures that cause human suffering and injustice; by denouncing injustices and speaking the truth to those in power; by acting in solidarity with the poor and the oppressed to change the causes of injustice.

In the latest social message, **A Society to be Transformed,** the Canadian bishops again urged Christian communities to become involved in struggles for justice. The bishops' message outlined plans for pastoral programmes designed to strengthen the Church's ministry for justice and the transformation of society. The programme itself involved the preparation of a primer or working instruments on social and economic justice, the formation of local study-action groups on injustices in Canada and the Third World, and the organization of conferences or seminars at diocesan or regional levels. This programme was to be developed and implemented over a period of several years in the Church.

The bishops and the staff of the CCCB's Social Affairs Commission have been given the primary responsibility for developing this pastoral programme. As our first major task, we have prepared this primer or set of working instruments for justice. The purpose of this primer is to assist Christian communities in developing their ministry for justice. It is a resource guide for Christian animators — priests, lay leaders, religious, school teachers, and others — who are concerned about developing study-action programmes for justice and the transformation of society.

This primer consists of three working papers. Each is designed to stimulate critical awareness, action, and reflection on the realities of injustice in our society and that of the Third World.

(1)   **Faith and Justice:** A background paper for Christian animators outlining the basis for developing a pastoral programme of education and action in response to injustice in Canada and the Third World. This paper takes up the following topics: demands for justice in the Third World and Canada and their impact on the social teachings of the Church; the relation between faith and justice, liberation and salvation; the prophetic mission of the Church and the prophetic witness of Christians; a framework for developing a critical awareness on injustices in Canada and the Third World, and some methods or tools that may be used in developing programmes for education and action.

(2)   **Justice in Canada:** A resource guide for Christian animators concerned about developing critical awareness of social and economic injustices in our own society. This working instrument deals with such topics as: the economic order, political order, continuing poverty, industrial exploitation; production and human needs; regional development; community development; northern development; social controls; minority discrimination; and consumer society.

In reference to these topics, this instrument attempts to list some resource materials which may be useful for study and animation, to identify some Christian education and action programmes on specific issues of injustice, and to pose questions for reflection on the part of Christian animators.

(3)   **Justice in the Third World:** A resource guide for Christian animators concerned about developing critical awareness of social and economic injustices in the Third World and Canada's relationship to these problems. The working instrument deals with such topics as: historical underdevelopment of the Third World; the global economic order; self-reliant development; foreign aid; international trade; foreign investment; world hunger; repression of human rights; military armament; immigration and refugee policies. In reference to these topics, this instrument also attempts to list some resource materials which may be useful for study and animation, to identify some Christian education and action programmes on specific issues of injustice in the Third World, and to pose some questions for reflection on the part of Christian animators.

Together, these working instruments have been prepared to assist Christian animators in developing study and action programmes on social and economic justice. As such, they are not meant to be used for direct animation with groups. Instead, they are primarily designed to assist animators themselves in developing their own projects during the course of the next few years. It is also important to note that these working instruments are not meant to be complete or comprehensive. They are part of an ongoing process in Christian communities in which people are engaged in developing critical analysis, awareness, and action on the issues of injustice. Thus, animators who use these working instruments are encouraged to further refine and develop the contents of this primer on the basis of their own experiences.

It should also be noted that the resource materials and action projects identified in these working instruments reflect different perspectives for analyzing and transforming our socio-economic order. In addressing specific problems of injustice, some of the materials and projects reflect a concern to reform capitalism, others employ Marxist tools of analysis, and still others attempt to use alternative perspectives. Given this pluralism, there are bound to be some differences and contradictions in the analysis of various issues. At the same time, the resource materials identified here do not necessarily represent the policies or positions of the bishops. They are offered to animators for information purposes.

Finally, in preparing the primer we have tried to reflect the variety of options and strategies open to Christian communities engaged in struggles for justice. As the Canadian bishops concluded their last message:

"In your neighbourhood you may be faced with a variety of options and strategies. Some people will choose to continue reforming our present capitalist system in the light of the Gospel. Others will choose to participate in socialist movements, trying to reconcile them with the teachings of Jesus. And still others, rejecting these options, will become involved in searching for some alternative socio-economic order based on Gospel principles. As people pursue these different strategies, there is bound to be within the Christian community tension and debate which can be a healthy process for change. But one thing is certain: No option is valid that does not unite people in efforts for the creation of a society based on justice."

Most Reverend John Sherlock
President
Social Affairs Department
Canadian Conference of Catholic Bishops

Most Reverend Bernard Hubert
Chairman
Episcopal Commission for Social Affairs
Canadian Conference of Catholic Bishops

*The Social Affairs Commission is composed of the following bishops: Austin E. Burke, bishop of Yarmouth, Nova Scotia; Remi J. De Roo, bishop of Victoria, British Columbia; Jean-Guy Hamelin, bishop of Rouyn-Noranda, Québec; Bernard Hubert, bishop of Saint-Jean-de-Québec, Québec; John O'Mara, bishop of Thunder Bay, Ontario; Adolphe Proulx, bishop of Hull, Québec; John Sherlock, bishop of London, Ontario; Peter Sutton, bishop of Labrador-Schefferville, Québec.

The staff of the Social Affairs Commission includes the following: M. l'abbé Aubert April, Pastoral Team member; Tony Clarke, director, Social Affairs Desk; Bernard Daly, Pastoral Team member; Bernard Dufresne, research assistant, Normand Paquin, directeur, Bureau des affaires sociales. The secretariat also includes Elaine Hopson and Louisette Villeneuve-Arnal.

NOTE:

The documents resulting from the Puebla Conference and Pope John Paul II's encyclical, **Redemptor Hominis,** were released at the time of publication of this text. Together, these documents reaffirm and strengthen the prophetic mission of the Church for justice and the transformation of society. Due to printing schedules, however, it was possible only to make passing reference to these important documents in this text.

MULTI-MEDIA KIT

The Canadian Religious Conference has prepared a multi-media kit for Christian animators based on the three working instruments. The kit contains several slide-tape documentaries which may be useful for initial animation in parishes, schools, and community groups.

The multi-media kit includes one slide-tape presentation on the basic themes of the working instruments and five other slide-tape documentaries on specific issues and regions. The first presentation (10 minutes) provides an overview of the three themes (Faith and Justice, Justice in Canada, Justice in the Third World) and illustrates this by focusing attention on the work of Christians in the struggles of Native people in Labrador and peasant farmers in the Dominican Republic. The other five documentaries highlight the work of Christians on specific issues of social and economic justice in different regions of the country: (i) fishermen in Newfoundland (10 minutes); (ii) industrial workers in Quebec (12 minutes); (iii) the elderly in Ontario (10 minutes); (iv) uranium development in Saskatchewan (10 minutes); (v) Native people and pipeline construction in the Yukon and British Columbia (10 minutes).

Copies of the kit (in whole or in part) are available on order:

En français:

Bible Centre Biblique
2000, rue Sherbrooke ouest
Montréal, P.Q.
H3H 1G4

In English:

Life Cycle Books
4 Richmond Street East
Suite 425
Toronto, Ontario
M5C 1M6

FAITH
AND
JUSTICE

Introduction

In recent years, a growing number of Christians in the Catholic community have committed themselves to the struggle for justice in the world. For the most part, this form of Christian activity has come in response to increasing awareness of injustices in both Canada and the Third World. At the same time, the bishops of Canada have attempted to reflect on these experiences and clarify some new directions in the theology and mission of the Church, through various Labour Day messages and pastoral statements. As a result, some insights have emerged for the further development of a pastoral programme for justice and the transformation of society.

This chapter is designed to provide a general introduction to such a pastoral programme. It is divided into four parts. Part one reflects briefly on the impact of the growing demands for justice in the Third World and Canada on the social teachings and pastoral programmes of the Church in recent years. Part two takes up some recent theological themes concerning the relationship between faith and justice, liberation and salvation. Part three attempts to clarify some dimensions of the prophetic mission of the Church and the prophetic witness of Christians for justice. Part four proposes a framework for developing a critical analysis of our society, outlines a pastoral programme for education and action, and describes some tools and places for animation in Christian communities.

This chapter is, therefore, designed to introduce a pastoral programme. It provides a background for two working instruments: one on Justice in Canada, the other on Justice in the Third World. It also serves as a resource guide for Christian animators. Each part includes a list of resource materials that may be used for study and animation. In addition, a more comprehensive list of resource materials is included at the end of this chapter.*

Finally, it should be noted that this chapter suggests a framework for theological reflection on action for justice and liberation. It is clear, however, that this chapter does not provide a comprehensive treatment of the wide range of ethical and theological themes related to justice. Certain themes and resources have been identified here because they help to illustrate some of the major trends in Christian thought and action concerning justice and liberation. Animators, however, are encouraged to do their own theological reflection in relation to specific experiences of active engagement in struggles for justice. In doing so, animators will want to make use of the Scriptures and the social teachings of the Church to identify appropriate ethical and theological themes for reflection on specific action experiences.

*Except for official Church documents, the resource materials are generally in alphabetical order.

I. Demands for Justice

The Second Vatican Council generated a new spirit in the life of the Catholic Church. Following Vatican II, in pursuit of her spiritual mission, the Church re-oriented her pastoral priorities to serve the needs of people in the world and respond to the human struggles for justice and dignity. Since Vatican II, the demands for justice voiced by people suffering from conditions of poverty and oppression throughout the world have had a major impact on both the social teaching and the pastoral programme of the Church. In this context, Part I will touch on some initial reflections concerning (a) the demands for justice in the Third World and (b) the demands for justice here in Canada.

Demands for Justice ... in the Third World

"There is also the scandal of glaring inequalities not merely in the enjoyment of possessions but even more in the exercise of power. While a small restricted group enjoys a refined civilization in certain regions, the remainder of the population, poor and scattered, is 'deprived of nearly all possibility of personal initiative and of responsibility, and often times even its living and working conditions are unworthy of the human person' (Gaudium et Spes, No. 63, Par. 3)".
(Paul VI, Populorum Progressio, No. 9, 1967)

"The serious injustices ... are building around the world of men a network of domination, oppression, and abuses which stifle freedom and which keep the greater part of humanity from sharing in the building up and the enjoyment of a more just and fraternal world."
(Third Synod of Bishops, Justice in the World, No. 3, 1971)

The harsh realities of poverty and oppression are to be found in all parts of the world today, especially in the Third World countries of Africa, Asia, and Latin America. For example:

—two thirds of all human beings on this earth lack adequate food, housing, clothing, education, employment, and other basic human needs;

—close to 500 million people are suffering from starvation, malnutrition and disease;

—the gap between the rich and poor countries continues to grow despite the United Nations first and second Development Decade programmes;

—the resources, often non-renewable, of most Third World countries are exploited to serve the interests of the industrialized nations rather than the basic needs of their own populations;

—the purchasing power of poor countries continues to decline because of the unequal terms of trade on world markets;

—large transnational corporations are increasingly gaining control over the economies of many Third World countries;

4

—mounting debt problems and spiralling inflation have virtually crippled the social and economic life of the poorest countries;

—the growth of military regimes in Latin America, South East Asia, and Africa have resulted in the imprisonment, torture and death of countless numbers of people.

Social Teachings

The increasing demands for justice in the Third World have had a major impact on the social teachings of the Church itself. The Kingdom of God itself is a gift of Christ. Yet, the Church has a vital role to play in preparing for the Kingdom by working for the elimination of poverty, oppression, and misery throughout the world. At Vatican II, the bishops of Latin America, Africa, and Asia stressed the pastoral problems that arise from the realities of poverty and oppression in the Third World reflected on them in **Gaudium et Spes.** In 1967, Pope Paul VI issued his encyclical **Populorum Progressio,** in which he argued that the growing gap between the rich and the poor, the powerful and the powerless, posed a serious threat to the survival of mankind. Referring to the times as "an hour of crisis", Paul VI challenged Christians to become actively involved in changing the structures that cause the underdevelopment of peoples.

In the following year, the **Medellin Conference** of the Latin American bishops denounced the "institutionalized violence" of the status quo, and placed responsibility for injustice in Latin America on those with "greater share of wealth, culture and power". In 1971, Paul VI's apostolic letter to Cardinal Roy, **Octogesima Adveniens** focused attention again on the injustices of poverty and oppression and outlined guidelines for political action on the part of Christians. Soon after, the Third Synod of the bishops on **Justice in the World** further clarified the pastoral priorities of the Church in responding to the demands of justice and liberation, particularly in reference to the poor and oppressed peoples of Third World countries. And the Fourth Synod on **Evangelization in the Modern World** stressed the relationship between the Church's mission of proclaiming the Gospel and the liberation and development of peoples.

Pastoral Programmes

In response to these demands, the Church has launched a variety of pastoral programmes over the past decade. In Latin America, for example, the bishops put a pastoral priority on defending the rights of the poor and oppressed and stimulating a "living awareness of justice" among their peoples. Since Medellin, the Church in Latin America has promoted "small base communities" in several countries to evangelize the marginal poor more effectively and to support them in their struggle for justice. In Canada as well, pastoral programmes have been developed in response to the demands for justice in the Third World. Through the Canadian Catholic Organization for Development and Peace, the Church has provided funds for specific development projects in Africa, Asia and Latin America. An extensive education programme has been implemented in Catholic parishes across the country concerning the problems and causes of underdevelopment in the Third World.

In addition, several action-research projects have been organized on an ecumenical basis to focus on specific problems such as: the structures of the global economic order that impede the development of Third World countries; the realities of world hunger and the problems of food production; the growing repression of human rights in the military regimes of Latin America, Africa, and South East Asia; the arms race and build-up of military regimes in various Third World countries; expanding population growth and the problems posed by restrictive immigration and refugee policies in western industrialized countries. The role of the Canadian government and Canadian transnational corporations in relation to the continuing poverty and oppression in Third World countries has been a major pastoral concern for these projects.

Some References:

Between Honesty and Hope, Orbis Books, Maryknoll, New York, 1970.

A collection of documents from and about the Church in Latin America. Available on order from your Catholic bookstore or your local bookstore.

de Montvalon, R., **Trois encycliques sociales,** Seuil, Paris, 1967, 252 pages.

Un recueil des trois encycliques, Mater et Magistra, Pacem in Terris, Populorum Progressio, présentées et annotées par l'auteur. Disponible en librairie.

Gremillion, J., **Gospel of Justice and Peace,** Orbis Books, Maryknoll, New York, 1978, 622 pages.

A collection of the Church's major social teaching documents in recent years, including: Pacem in Terris, Mater et Magistra, Gaudium et Spes (excerpts), Populorum Progressio, Medillin Documents, Octogesima Adveniens, Justice in the World, plus statements made by Pope Paul VI at such events as the World Food Conference. Available on order from your local bookstore.

Pontifical Commission for Justice and Peace, **The Church and Human Rights,** Vatican City, 1976, 71 pages.

A précis on the Church's social teachings with respect to human rights. Available on order from your Catholic bookstore.

Demands For Justice ...
... in Canada

"We live in a world that oppresses at least half the human race and this scandal threatens to get worse. Right around us, human suffering of many kinds scars the human face of Canada; poverty for many, inflating prices, housing crisis, regional disparities, strikes and lockouts, cultural violations, Native land claims, overcrowded cities, and rural neglect. With all this comes a growing sense of loneliness, powerlessness, and alienation in our society and institutions. But it is not enough to see injustice, disorder, and violence at home and abroad and to worry about the future. These conditions will not improve on their own. We, the people, have the responsibility to change them.
(Canadian Bishops, From Words to Action, *No. 1, 1976)*

In Canada, there are also demands for justice coming from people who are suffering from various forms of poverty and oppression. For example:

—industrial workers: in some cases have no control over the decisions affecting their social and economic well-being (e.g. plant shutdowns, while prices and profits keep rising);

—working poor: trying desperately to live and support their families on very low wages in the face of constant inflating prices;

—the jobless: more than a million people out of work, the highest rate of unemployment since the 1930's;

—welfare poor: along with the working poor now face government cutbacks in health care, education and social services;

—small producers: increasing numbers of small farmers and fishermen being forced out of business and their way of life by large corporations which now control markets and prices;

—Native people: still one of the most oppressed in this country, having the highest rates of unemployment, suicides, and infant mortality;

—immigrants: many poor people emigrating from other countries along with refugees fleeing from oppressive regimes are confronted with other social problems here in Canada;

—elderly people: those living on fixed incomes are confronted with the added burdens of inflation and cutbacks in social services;

—women: in spite of recent changes in public attitudes, many still experience discrimination in their family life and working place;

—cultural minorities: all over the country, francophone minorities and other cultural groups are constantly faced with problems of language rights and forms of cultural domination;

—racial minorities: who have emigrated from other countries for economic reasons have become the scapegoat for unemployment and related social problems in many of our cities;

—prisoners: their rights are often ignored in penitentiaries and when released they encounter major difficulties in adjusting and being accepted by society;

—children: possess very few rights recognized by law and are sometimes subjected to mental and bodily harm.

Social Teachings

The growing demands for justice in this country have had significant impact on the social teachings of the Church in Canada. In a series of annual Labour Day messages and pastoral statements, for example, the bishops of Canada have been engaged in a process of analyzing and commenting, from the standpoint of the Gospel, on the problems of justice facing our society. Through these statements, the bishops have spoken out on a range of social and economic issues: continuing poverty, exploitation of workers, relations between employers and workers, unemployment, immigration, food production, energy policies, housing problems, Native peoples, northern development, economic situation of families, consumerism, relations between Quebec and the rest of Canada and related questions of justice. In these statements, Christians have been encouraged, as an expression of their faith and commitment, to become actively involved in developing an ethical analysis of the problems and supporting the struggles of people to change the causes of injustice.

Pastoral Programmes

Responding to the demands for justice in our society, the Church has developed a variety of pastoral programmes in recent years. In several dioceses, for example, social justice programmes have been launched for the purpose of stimulating Christian education and action in parishes and communities. At national, regional, and local levels, there are a number of action-research projects on specific issues of social or economic justice, for example: the exploitation of workers in various industries; the struggle of northern Native people in the face of massive industrial development on their land, the plight of jobless people and the structural causes of unemployment; the problems faced by small farmers and small fishermen in food production; the continuing realities of poverty and the structures that maintain it; the various forms of cultural, racial and sexual discrimination; the deterioration of living conditions in urban and rural communities; the exploitation of resources and the underdevelopment of certain regions in the country; the erosion of democratic rights and civil liberties. In these kinds of pastoral programmes, a growing number of Christians have been putting their faith into practice by supporting poor and oppressed peoples in their struggle to change the causes of injustice, including the policies of governments and corporations.

Some References:

Arès R., s.j., **Messages des évêques canadiens à l'occasion de la Fête du Travail 1956-1974,** Editions Bellarmin, Montréal, 1974, 191 pages.

Recueil des messages des évêques canadiens de 1956 à 1974, présentés par l'auteur. Disponible en-librairie.

Justice Demands Action, Ten Days for World Development Publication, Toronto, 1976.

A popularized version of the brief presented by the leaders of Canada's major churches to the Federal Cabinet, March, 1976, on several issues of justice in Canada and the Third World. Includes information on some of the action-research projects of the churches. Available on order from Ten Days for World Development, 600 Jarvis Street, Toronto.

Ryan, M., **Christian Social Teaching and Canadian Society,** St Peter's Seminary, London, Ontario, 1978 (second edition).

A practical guide on the application of the Church's social teachings to socio-economic problems in our society. Available on order from St Peter's Seminary, Waterloo Street, London, Ontario, N6A 3Y1.

Witness to Justice, Development and Peace, Toronto, 1978.

A collection of some of the more recent social statements and messages by the Canadian bishops: Sharing Daily Bread (1974); Northern Development: At What Cost? (1975); From Words to Action (1976); A Society to be Transformed (1977). Available on order from Development and Peace, 67 Bond Street, Toronto, Ontario.

II. Justice and Liberation

The increasing involvement of Christians in concrete struggles for justice and liberation has posed some fundamental theological questions. What is the relationship between belief in God and action for justice? What is the Christian view of liberation and its relationship to salvation? In recent years, attempts have been made to clarify these and related questions. Part II, therefore, takes up some of the theological elements in (a) the relationship between faith and justice and (b) the relationship between liberation and salvation.

Justice and Faith

The uncertainty of history and the painful convergence in the ascending path of the human community direct us to sacred history; there God has revealed Himself to us and made known to us, as it is brought progressively to realization, His plan of liberation and salvation which is once and for all fulfilled in the Paschal mystery of Christ.

Action on behalf of justice and participation in the transformation of the world fully appear to us as a constitutive dimension of the preaching of the Gospel, or, in other words the Church's mission for the redemption of the human race and its liberation from every oppressive situation.
(Justice in the World, *No. 6, 1971*)

The Third Synod on Justice in the World emphasized that acting for justice is not an optional activity for Christians. It is integral to the proclamation of the Gospel and the practice of the Christian faith. Indeed, the struggle for justice and liberation is a major theme running through the Scriptures. (**Justice in the World,** p. 14).

Broken Covenant

For Christians, God intervened in history to eradicate the sins that destroy the covenant between man and God. The realities of injustice among people — the poverty, the hunger, the illness, the marginalization, the exploitation, the loss of dignity — are all signs of man's inhumanity to man and the broken covenant between God and man. In the midst of this broken covenant, God revealed Himself to be on the side of the poor, the oppressed, and the outcasts of society. In the tradition of the prophets, Yahweh is known as the God who especially loves and cares for the poor (eg. **Psalm** 12:5; **Isaiah** 25: 4). He is the God who defends and protects the poor and the weak (eg. **Deuteronomy** 15:4-11, 24:14-15; **Exodus** 22:22-25; **Leviticus** 19:13). For Yahweh is the God who will establish a reign of justice, where each is given according to his needs and where oppression is eliminated (**Isaiah** 9:6, **Psalm** 72).

Ministry of Jesus

Jesus Himself came to fulfil the covenant. At the inauguration of His ministry, Jesus announced that He was the message of the prophets come true, "good news to the poor" and "liberty to the oppressed" (**Luke 4:16-19; Luke 7:22; Matthew** 11:4-6). Throughout His ministry, He repeatedly identified with the plight of the poor, the afflicted, the oppressed and the outcasts of society (**Philippians** 2: 6-8). For Jesus, these people were open to salvation and blessed by God. (e.g. **Luke** 6: 20-21). At the same time, He took a critical attitude towards the accumulation of wealth and power that comes through the exploitation of others (e.g. **Luke** 16:13-15, 12:16-21; **Mark** 4:19). And, in the account of the great judgment, Jesus makes it quite clear that acceptance of Him is equated with loving one's neighbour and seeking justice for the poor, the afflicted and the oppressed (**Matthew** 25:31-46). For it is the just who will receive eternal life (**Matthew** 25:46).

Knowing God

But this teaching goes further. Jesus taught us that one way people can come to know and experience God more deeply is by loving others and seeking justice for the poor, the disinherited, the oppressed, the aged, the sick, and imprisoned (e.g. **Matthew** 25: 31-36; **Mark** 10: 42-45; **Luke** 4: 18-20; **John** 5: 7-8; **James** 2: 1-13, 5: 1-6). In doing so, Jesus stood in the tradition of the prophets of Israel who deepened their own understanding and knowledge of God by defending the cause of the poor and the oppressed (e.g. **Amos; Jeremiah; Isaiah; Micah; Hosea; Psalms** 9, 10, 40, 72, 76, 146). Indeed, the prophets themselves believed that he who does not defend the cause of the poor and the oppressed, does not really know God (**Hosea** 4:1). For he who does not live in the defence of his brothers does not live in the light (**I John:** 2: 9-11, 3: 16-17). Thus, people can deepen their knowledge of God and grow in their faith through participation with the poor and the oppressed in their struggles for justice.

Love and Justice

The Christian Gospel of love, therefore, "implies an absolute demand for justice" (**Justice in the World,** No. 34). Indeed, justice is the political arm of love. It seeks the transformation of unjust attitudes and structures so that society may serve the needs of all people for a more fully human life. Thus, justice is not charity, namely, giving alms to the poor. Seeking justice involves conversion of hearts and actions to change social, economic and political structures that cause human suffering. The Gospel teaches us, however, that people must seek justice with love and compassion for those who are suffering. This, in turn, requires that people see reality from the perspective of Jesus and His liberating concern for the poor and the oppressed.

Justice in the World

For Christians, the living God of history is the Lord of Justice. All persons are made in the image of God. And, therefore, our dignity as persons confers on us certain inalienable rights. Of primary importance is the right to life and all that renders life possible such as food, clothing, shelter, education, employment and health care (e.g. **Gaudium et Spes,** No. 26; **Pacem in Terris,** No. 8-26). At the same time, people have the right to self-determination, to define their own future, and to participate in decisions affecting their lives (**Populorum Progressio; Justice in the World**). Thus, the primary purpose of economic development is to serve the needs of people in a given society. The resources of the earth are to be developed to serve the common good, namely, the needs of all people for a more fully human life (**Gaudium et Spes,** No. 63) and "all other rights whatsoever, including those of property and free commerce, are to be subordinated to this principle" (**Populorum Progressio,** No. 22).

Structures of Injustice

In its recent social teachings, the Church draws particular attention to social structures which cause injustice in the world. The operations of social, economic and political institutions that result in human suffering are identified as "structures of injustice". The unjust systems and structures which subject masses of people in a state of poverty and oppression throughout the world today, constitute a "grave sin of injustice" (**Justice in the World,** No. 29). In our times, for example, certain transnational corporations have accumulated a great deal of economic power and for this reason have been referred to in terms of the "new imperialism of money" (**Octogesima Adveniens,** No. 44). As a result, governments are often incapable of serving human needs and promoting the common good. This is why the social teachings of the Church have developed a more and more critical perspective in regard to economic systems such as liberal capitalism (**Populorum Progressio,** No. 26) and its structures of domination and injustice.

Some References:

Third Synod of Bishops, **Justice in the World,** Vatican City, 1975.

The principal document of the 1971 World Synod of Bishops outlining Christian responsibilities for justice in the world. Full text available in the **Gospel of Peace and Justice** (Orbis Books, Maryknoll, New York, 1976).

Alfaro, J., **Theology of Justice in the World,** Pontifical Commission for Justice and Peace, Vatican City, 1971.

A follow-up document to the Third Synod of Bishops outlining some theological elements in relation to justice in the world. Available on order from your Catholic bookstore or library.

Cosmao, V., **Développement et Foi,** Paris, Editions du Cerf, 1972.

Une étude sur la relation entre la foi, la justice et le développement des peuples. Disponible en librairie.

Eagleson, J., Scharpner, B., **The Radical Bible,** Maryknoll, New York, 1972.

The gospel's radical message of social justice juxtapozed with voices from the Third World describing their reality. Available on order from your local bookstore or library.

Haughey, J., **The Faith that Does Justice,** Paulist Press, New York, 1977, 290 pages.

A collection of articles examining the Christian sources for social justice and social change. Available on order from your Catholic bookstore or library.

Miranda, J., **Marx and the Bible** (A Critique of the Philosophy of Oppression), Orbis Books, Maryknoll, New York, 1974, 338 pages.

An in-depth study of the scriptural foundations concerning Christian action for justice. Available on order from your local bookstore or library.

Torres and Fabella ed., **The Emergent Gospel,** Orbis Books, Maryknoll, New York, 1978.

The official report of the Third Conference of theologians in Dar es Salaam (1976), including a statement on method and theological objectives regarding justice and liberation.

Liberation and Salvation

The very God who creates men in his image and likeness is the same God who, in the fullness of time, sends His son in the flesh, so that He might come to liberate all men from the slavery to which sin has subjected them: hunger, misery, oppression, and ignorance, in a word that injustice and hatred which have their origins in human selfishness.
(Medellin Documents, *Justice, 1968)*

The Church strives always to insert the Christian struggle for liberation into the universal plan of salvation which she herself proclaims.
(Evangelization in the Modern World, *No. 38,1975)*

11

The Third Synod, largely inspired by the experience of the Church in Latin America, emphasized that justice demands the liberation of people from the realities of poverty, oppression, and underdevelopment. And the Fourth Synod went on to clarify the Christian struggle for liberation in the context of the universal plan for salvation proclaimed by Christ.

Social Sin

The recent teachings of the Church have pointed out the realities of social sin in our times. The social structures and attitudes which keep people poor, hungry and powerless throughout the world are prime examples of social sin today. They violate God's purpose for man and contradict His plan for creation (**Justice in the World,** No. 5). These are the social consequences of the personal sin of human selfishness and greed. In the Scriptures, it is God's will to deliver His people from the evil conditions which separate God and man.

Justice and Liberation

The Good News announced by Christ simultaneously involved liberation from the misery of poverty and oppression and the proclamation of God's Kingdom in Heaven. It is through participation in actions for justice that people can be liberated, especially in struggles to change the social, economic and political structures that cause human suffering. Thus, participation in the struggles for justice provides opportunities for people to collaborate with the saving power of Christ, in their own salvation and that of their neighbours, thereby preparing the way for the Kingdom that is to come.

Liberation and Development

In concrete situations, the Christian view of liberation emphasizes the self-determination of peoples. It stresses the potential of human beings to take control of their own destinies (**Justice in the World,** No. 17). Thus the Church's teaching flatly rejects colonial models of development wherein a powerful few take control of people and resources of a given society (**Populorum Progressio,** No. 52; **Justice in the World,** No. 16). Moreover, models of development primarily based on expanding economic growth and technological manipulation rather than integral human development, are also considered inadequate for human liberation. Instead, the Church emphasizes models of development based on self-reliance, responsible nationalism, and the participation of people in social, economic and political decisions and plans affecting their lives (**Justice in the World,** No. 17, 18; **Populorum Progression,** No. 34).

True Liberation

The Christian view of liberation, however, includes but goes beyond fundamental changes in the social, economic, and political structures that oppress people. True liberation encompasses the whole person and opens men and women to God and his plan for the salvation of mankind. This openness to God allows people to see the limits of their human activity. It forces people to search for a greater liberation, namely, that gift of eternal freedom that comes "in the joy of knowing God and being known by him, of seeing him, and of being given over to him". (**Evangelization in the Modern World,** No. 9).

Kingdom of God

Thus, the Christian struggle for liberation is inserted into the universal plan for salvation proclaimed by Christ. (**Evangelization in the Modern World,** No. 38). In announcing that the Kingdom of God was at hand (e.g. **Matthew** 4:17, 23), Jesus proclaimed the Good News for the salvation of mankind from the sins of the world. Through the Kingdom, Christ promised that people who "put on the new self" (**Ephesians** 4:24, 2:15) would be "reconciled to God" (**2 Corinthians** 5:20) their father in heaven (e.g. **Matthew** 8:11ff, 13:43, 26:29).

Christ's Liberating Power

The liberating power of Christ, as symbolized in his death and resurrection, frees people from the sins of the world and opens them up to communion with God. The Kingdom belongs to those who "put on the new self" and open themselves up to communion with God by struggling against the sins of injustice that continue to separate God and man. Because of their own experience, Jesus declared that the poor, the destitute, the oppressed are more open to God and would inherit the Kingdom (**Matthew** 5: 3-10, 11:5; **Luke** 4:18, 7:22, 14:13; **James** 2:5). At the same time, he warned the wealthy and the powerful of the difficulties they would face in entering God's Kingdom (**Luke** 16: 19-31; **Luke** 18:24-27).

Liberating Events

The Kingdom of God, which Christ inaugurated, is already present yet still to come. Jesus called on all God's people to share in the preparation for the coming of the Kingdom. This entails participation in the struggle of the poor and the oppressed for justice and liberation. Indeed, wherever people are involved in struggles against the injustices suffered by the poor, the hungry, the sick, the marginalized, the exploited and other oppressed peoples, they are engaged in liberating events. It is through such liberating events that growth in the coming Kingdom takes place and salvation from the sins of the world is made possible.

Some References:

Paul VI, **Evangelization in the Modern World,** Vatican City, 1975.

Pope Paul VI's statement summarizing the latest teaching of the Church on liberation and salvation, based on the 1974 World Synod of Bishops. Available at cost on order from the Publication Service, Canadian Conference of Catholic Bishops, 90 Parent Avenue, Ottawa, Ontario, K1N 7B1.

Boff, L., **Jésus-Christ Libérateur,** Editions du Cerf, Paris, 1974.

Un ouvrage sur Jésus dans le cadre de la théologie de la libération. Disponible en librairie.

Dussel, E., **History and the Theology of Liberation,** Orbis Books, Maryknoll, New York, 1976.

A well-documented account of the emergence of liberation theology in the Latin American experience. Available on order from your local bookstore or library.

Giguère, P.A. et alii, **Cri de Dieu, espoir des pauvres,** Editions Paulines, Montréal, 1977.

Un ouvrage sur la pauvreté et sa signification biblique. Disponible en bibliothèque.

Gutierrez, G., **A Theology of Liberation,** Orbis Books, Maryknoll, New York, 1973.

A challenging presentation of the theology of liberation by one of its leading exponents. Available on order from your local bookstore or library.

International Theological Commission, **Declaration on Human Development and Christian Salvation,** Vatican City, 1975, 15 pages.

The report of the International Theological Commission on liberation and salvation. Available on order from the Publication Office, United States Catholic Conference, 1312 Massachussetts Avenue N.W., Washington, D.C. 20005.

Laurentin R., **Liberation, Development and Salvation,** Orbis Books, Maryknoll, New York, 1973.

Explores the impact of the Third World on the Church's theology for justice and liberation. Available on order from your local bookstore or library.

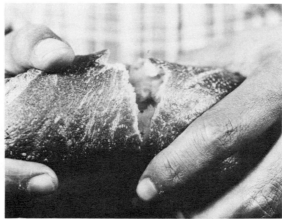

III. Mission of the Church

The participation of Christians in struggles for justice and liberation has also raised questions about the mission of the Church. How does the Church understand its mission of proclaiming the Good News and seeking justice for the poor and the oppressed? What is the specific role of Christians in the struggle for justice and liberation? Attempts have been made in recent years to clarify these and related questions. Part III identifies some of the themes that have emerged in recent social teachings concerning the prophetic mission of the Church and the prophetic witness of Christians.

Prophetic Mission of the Christian Community

Listening to the cry of those who suffer violence and are oppressed by unjust systems and structures, and hearing the appeal of a world that by its perversity contradicts the plan of its Creator, we have shared our awareness of the Church's vocation to be present in the heart of the world by proclaiming the Good News to the poor, freedom to the oppressed, and joy to the afflicted.
(Justice in the World, *No. 5, 1971*)

At the same time as it proclaims the Gospel of the Lord, its Redeemer and Saviour, the Church calls on all, especially the poor, the oppressed, and the afflicted, to cooperate with God to bring about liberation from every sin and to build a world which will reach the fullness of creation only when it becomes the work of man for man.
(Justice in the World, *No. 77, 1971*)

The Third Synod clarified some major elements in the prophetic mission of the Church. The Synod emphasized that it was the prophetic mission of the Church to proclaim the Good News of God's Kingdom through active participation in the struggle of the poor and the oppressed for justice and liberation.

Prophetic Tradition

The Christian community today is the inheritor of a deeply rooted prophetic tradition. Central to this prophetic tradition is the activity of bearing witness to the struggle of the poor and the oppressed. Guided by the Holy Spirit, the prophets of Israel repeatedly denounced the injustices of their time and called for the creation of a new society based on equality and justice for mankind. And Jesus, inspired by the same Spirit, proclaimed the coming of God's Kindgom. Identifying with the plight of the poor, the oppressed and the afflicted, Jesus offered mankind new hope for liberation from the sins of injustice.

Early Church

The early Church continued the mission of Christ, proclaiming the Good News to the poor and looking for concrete signs of the coming Kingdom. In Jerusalem, the early Church stressed the communal sharing of resources to serve the needs of the poor and the outcasts of society (**Acts** 2: 44-45, 4: 32). Elsewhere, Paul called on the early Christian to embody the special care of God for the poor and the poverty of Christ (2 **Corinthians** 9:9, 8:9) and emphasized the principle of equality (2 **Corinthians** 8:14). Although experiencing "extreme poverty" itself, the Macedonian Church is reported to have joyfully participated in sharing and assisting those who were poor (2 **Corinthians** 8:13-15). For the early Christians, therefore, faith in Jesus Christ required identification with the plight of the poor and the oppressed and rejection of individual wealth as an impediment to the Kingdom (e.g. **James** 2:1-7; **Philippians** 2:6-8).

Justice and Liberation

As the inheritors of this prophetic tradition, Jesus called on the people of God to share in the task of preparing for the coming Kingdom. In doing so, the Church is called to respond to the cries of the poor and the oppressed by participating in the struggle for justice and liberation. Indeed, it is through active participation in these struggles for justice and liberation that the Church can fulfil its mission of proclaiming the Good News of God's Kingdom to mankind. Unless the Christian community is actively engaged in this way, the Good News of salvation promised by God's Kingdom will lack credibility.

Transforming Society

The Christian community, therefore, is called to actively participate in the transformation of society. To do so, Christians must develop a critical awareness of the causes of injustice and participate in actions to change the social, economic, and political structures that cause human suffering. Thus, the participation of Christians in political action is a major aspect of the prophetic mission of the Church (**Octogesima Adveniens,** No. 24, No. 46). The transformation of society requires that people come together to bring about social and economic change. In some cases, the demands for justice and liberation may require Christians to be actively involved in changing the social and economic order itself.

Participation of Poor and Oppressed

The poor, the oppressed, and the afflicted have a major role to play in the prophetic mission of the Church concerning the transformation of society. Today, as in the case of the early Church, they comprise the majority of the Church's population in many places, particularly in the Third World. Yet the Church cannot be "a haven for the masses". Indeed, the poor and the oppressed are being called today to give leadership in the Church's mission for justice and liberation (**Justice in the World,** No. 77). At the same time, the Church can assist the poor and oppressed peoples in creating their own organizations in order to assure their own authentic liberation.

Liturgical Life

The liturgy, itself, has a major role to play in the prophetic mission of the Christian community. The liturgy of the Word can help Christians discover the teachings of the prophets, Christ, and the apostles and assist them in reflecting on the deeper meanings of their actions for justice in the light of God's plan for liberation and salvation. At the same time, the Eucharist, which forms the center of the Christian community, provides the occasion for celebrating the Paschal mystery of Christ, in which Christians find the central purpose for living the Gospel message of love and justice (**Justice in the World,** No. 34).

Some References:

Justice in the World (especially articles 35 to 48) and Paul VI, **Evangelization in the Modern World.**

Bigo, P., **The Church in Third World Revolution,** Orbis Books, Maryknoll, New York, 1977, 316 pages.

An analysis of the role of the Church in response to the demands for justice and liberation in the Third World. Available on order from you local bookstore or library.

Grand' Maison, J., **Crise de prophétisme,** l'Action catholique canadienne, Montréal, 1965, 315 pages.

Une réflexion sur les changements structuraux à apporter au sein de l'Eglise pour que celle-ci soit plus apte à comprendre et à accompagner la société contemporaine. Disponible en bibliothèque.

Gutierrez, G., **Réinventer le visage de l'Eglise,** les Editions du Cerf, Paris, 1971, 92 pages.

Une description et une analyse théologique de l'évolution de la pastorale en Amérique latine et en Europe. Disponible en librairie.

Houtart, Rousseau, **The Church and Revolution,** Orbis Books, Maryknoll, New York, 1970.

An analysis of the Church's response to revolutionary movements in different periods of history. Available on order from your local bookstore or library.

Segundo, L., **Hidden Motives of Pastoral Action,** Orbis Books, Maryknoll, New York, 1978.

An analysis of the Church's role in announcing and constructing the Kingdom of God in universal human history. Available on order from your local bookstore or library.

Prophetic Witness of Christians

The mission of preaching the Gospel dictates at the present time that we should dedicate ourselves to the liberation of man even in his present existence in this world. For unless the Christian message of love and justice shows its effectiveness through action in the cause of justice in the world, it will only with difficulty gain credibility with the men of our times.
(**Justice in the World**, *No. 35, 1971*)

*The message of Christ crucified is not a comforting message. We cannot take refuge in the position that, as Christians, our duty is simply to worship God and give alms to the poor (***Matthew** *7:21-23). To do this alone in the present situation would be to incur the wrath of Christ because, like the Pharisees, we would be neglecting "justice and the love of God" (***Luke** *11:42).*
(From Words to Action, *No. 10, 1976*)

Through the teachings of the Third Synod of bishops and Pope Paul VI's apostolic letter **Octogesima Adveniens,** insights have emerged concerning the prophetic witness of Christians for justice in the world today. The Canadian bishops' pastoral letter, **"From Words to Action",** further clarified the prophetic tasks for Christians.

Signs of the Kingdom

The authentic struggles for justice and liberation going on in the world today reveal that the Kingdom is already present yet still to come. They both illustrate and contribute to the coming of the Kingdom. Indeed, they are signs of hope for mankind. For, it is here in the midst of these struggles that Christians, in transforming society, proclaim the Gospel and bear witness to what the Church believes. In doing so, they maintain the vital link between salvation offered today by God and its final accomplishment. Indeed the work of Christians on earth prepares the way for heavenly Kingdom (**Gaudium et Spes,** No. 39).

Discerning the Signs

Discerning the signs of the Kingdom, therefore, is part of the prophetic task of Christians. This entails listening to the demands for justice of the poor and the oppressed in every concrete situation. It also entails developing a critical awareness of the sins which cause injustice in a particular situation. And it also requires prayer in order to discern the Word of God and the direction in which the Holy Spirit is leading. Through these tasks, the Christian can begin to discern how to bear witness to the signs of the Kingdom through participation in particular struggles for justice and liberation.

Being Present

The prophetic task also requires active presence with the poor and the oppressed. Indeed, a new vision of reality can be acquired by becoming more present with the hungry, the homeless, the jobless, the exploited worker, and others who are the victims of injustice. By listening to their problems and sharing in their struggle, Christians can learn a great deal more about the realities of poverty, oppression, and underdevelopment. Active presence is, therefore, imperative for the credibility of Christian witness to the Gospel message of love and justice.

Acting in Solidarity

Action, in solidarity with people engaged in struggles for justice and liberation, is a major part of the prophetic task of Christians. In doing so, it is essential to recognize that the poor and the oppressed themselves are the agents of their own liberation. Those Christian communities which are largely composed of the poor, the oppressed or the afflicted have a vital role to play in the struggle for liberation from the sins that cause injustice. At the same time, other Christian communities can play an important role by participating with the poor and the oppressed in changing the social, economic, and political structures that cause human suffering.

Theological Reflection

Theological reflection is an essential part of the prophetic witness of Christians. This involves taking the Word of God and applying it to the concrete realities of life. The Scriptures themselves and the social teachings of the Church provide basic resources for Christians to reflect theologically on their experiences of acting for justice. Indeed, reflecting on the experience of acting in solidarity with the poor and the oppressed can illuminate the ultimate purpose and meaning of peoples' struggles in particular moments of history.

Some References:

Paul VI, **Octogesima Adveniens,** Apostolic letter to Cardinal Maurice Roy, Vatican City, 1971.

Pope Paul VI's call to action that inaugurated the Pontifical Commission for Justice and Peace. Full text available in **Gospel of Justice and Peace** (Orbis Books, Maryknoll, New York, 1976).

Canadian bishops, **From Words to Action,** Canadian Conference of Catholic Bishops, Labour Day message, 1976.

This statement outlines some practical steps for Christians to become engaged in struggles for justice as a form of prophetic witness. Text available at cost on order from the Publication Service, Canadian Conference of Catholic Bishops, 90 Parent Avenue, Ottawa, Ontario, K1N 7B1.

Arrupe, P., s.j. **Witnessing to Justice,** Pontifical Commission for Justice and Peace, Vatican City, 1972, 63 pages.

One of the follow-up documents to the Third Synod of Bishops, this booklet provides some sights on the prophetic witness of Christians in the world. Available on order from your local Catholic bookstore.

de Broucker, J., **The Violence of a Peace Maker: Dom Helder Camara,** Orbis Books, Maryknoll, New York, 1970.

An engaging profile on the prophetic witness of one of the more controversial bishops in Latin America. Available on order from your local bookstore or library.

Lamont, D., **Speech from the Dock,** London, Kevin Matthew Ltd., 1977, 143 pages.

A portrayal of the prophetic witness of Bishop Lamont in opposing the racist regimes of Rhodesia and South Africa. Available on order from your local Catholic bookstore or library.

Syder, R., **Rich Christians in a Hungry World,** Paulist Press, New York, 1974.

A book challenging Christians in affluent, industrialized countries to take a critical look at the problems of poverty and hunger in the world from the perspective of the Gospel message. Available on order from your local bookstore or library.

IV. Transforming Society

It is up to each Christian community "to analyze with objectivity the situation which is proper to their own country, to shed on it the light of the Gospel's unalterable words and to draw principles of reflection, norms of judgment and directions for action from the social teachings of the Church."
(Paul VI, Octogesima Adveniens, *No. 4, 1971)*

The growing demands for justice in both Canada and the Third World have posed a major challenge to the prophetic mission of the Christian community in this country. The time has come, however, to deepen and strengthen our pastoral committment and action for the purpose of bringing about fundamental transformation in the economic and social structures that cause human suffering and injustice. The purpose of Part IV is (a) to propose a general framework for developing a more critical analysis of our society and (b) to outline a pastoral programme for education and action, including some tools and methods for animation.

The Canadian Paradox

"The present economic order is characterized by the maldistribution of wealth and the control of resources by a small minority. In the Third World this order emerges from a history of colonialism. In Canada, in the words of the Senate Committee on Poverty, 'the economic system in which most Canadians prosper is the same system which creates poverty'. In both Canada and the Third World powerful corporations are planning the use of natural resources without the participation of the people who are most directly affected. Governments in the First, Second and Third Worlds often do not exercise their responsibility to protect people from these abuses of power. The human consequences of the present order are dependency, loss of human dignity, poverty and even starvation."
Canadian Church Leaders, Justice Demands Action, *1976.*

"In many such ways, our country is still profoundly marked by the founders of liberal capitalism ... The theory of the survival of the fittest leads many to accept widespread poverty and the concentration of wealth and power in the hands of a few. Industrial strategies are designed specifically to produce maximum gratification and profit, so that wasteful consumption is systematically promoted ... The result is clear: many are kept from achieving certain basic necessities while others, trapped in their wealth, find great difficulty in meeting God, in knowing the person of Jesus and living his message. Succeeding generations are drawn into a culture, into ways of thinking and behaving, alien to God's purpose."
Canadian Bishops, A Society to be Transformed, *1977.*

In recent years, the Canadian bishops have urged Christian communities to take a critical look at our own reality. The many contradictions of our society — wealth and poverty, power and powerlessness, happiness and loneliness, hope and despair, comfort and misery, participation and alienation — raise serious questions about our social, economic and political structures. What kind of society have we become? What responsibility do Canada and its institutions have in the development of the Third World? What are the common links between the causes of injustice in this country and injustices in the Third World?

A Double Paradox

A social analysis of the Canadian reality shows that we are living with a double paradox. In the first place, Canada is a relatively affluent, developed country enjoying the wealth and comforts of a modern industrialized society. Yet, it is also clear that Canada has forms of economic, social and cultural injustices that characterize the underdeveloped countries of the Third World. In the second place, Canada finds itself situated within the global economy in a position similar to that of some Third World countries and therefore shares similar economic and political problems. Yet, Canadian governments and corporations also participate along with other industrialized states in the exploitation of certain Third World countries. This double paradox is important for understanding the injustices in Canada and the Third World.

Injustices in Canada

Canada has been referred to as the richest, underdeveloped country in the world today. On the one hand, Canada is blessed with an abundance of rich resources — human, natural and material resources — required to develop an economy and a social order to serve the needs of all the people in this country. On the other hand, Canada bears all the marks of an underdeveloped society: continuing poverty for a quarter of our population; class divisions between rich and poor; inequitable distribution of goods such as food, housing, energy and other basic necessities; regional disparities, cultural domination and constraints. In the midst of these injustices, feelings of loneliness, powerlessness, and despair prevail among all sectors of our population: rich and poor, powerful and powerless.

Injustices in the Third World

Canada's relationship to the Third World illustrates another side of the paradox. On the one hand, Canada shares several important problems with countries in the Third World: high levels of foreign ownership and control, forms of economic dependency, a relatively weak industrial base, plus economic, social and cultural inequalities. On the other hand, Canadian-based corporations and financial institutions, supported by government programmes, have been accumulating wealth at the expense of several Third World countries primarily in the Carribean and Latin America. In short, Canada participates in the global economy which exploits the poor countries of the Third World.

Paradox of Capitalism

This double paradox, which takes on its own distinctive form in the Canadian experience, is not entirely unique. The paradox of development and underdevelopment is characteristic of capitalism itself. Indeed, development and underdevelopment have been two sides of the same coin in modern capitalism. Those who have control over capital for investment make the decisions which ultimately shape the patterns of development and underdevelopment in both Canada and the Third World. In capitalist societies, where many key sectors of the economy are owned and controlled by a small minority and priority is placed on the maximization of profits, the goal of serving human needs and the common good becomes secondary. The social consequences of such an economic system are uneven patterns of development, inequitable distribution of wealth and power, dependency and loss of human dignity.

A Pastoral Programme

"As Christians, we stand in the biblical tradition where to know God is to seek justice for the disinherited, the poor, and the oppressed. Therefore, we have a responsibility first, to challenge social and economic structures which cause poverty and underdevelopment and, secondly, to increase the capacity of the poor and the oppressed in their struggle for a just social order.
Canadian Bishops Letter to the Canadian Catholic Organization for Development and Peace on the Tenth Anniversary of Populorum Progressio and Development and Peace, *1977.*

"We wish to express in the strongest possible way our continued support for the growing number of Christians engaged in struggles for justice. In the next two years, we intend to initiate a pastoral plan of action for the purpose of encouraging more members of the Catholic community to become more actively involved in creating a socio-economic order based on justice. We, therefore, urge people in Christian communities to ... participate in study/action projects ... designed to stimulate greater Christian awareness and action in each region on the vital issues of injustice in Canada and the Third World.
Canadian bishops, A Society to be Transformed, *1977.*

The realites of the Canadian paradox give rise to a set of major pastoral problems for the Christian community in this country. It is evident, however, that only a relatively small fraction of the total resources of the Church in Canada have been devoted to these pastoral priorities. A great deal more attention must be given to the task of developing critical awareness, action, and reflection in a variety of Christian communities regarding the realities of injustice in both Canada and the Third World. The following is a general outline of a pastoral programme for education and action that may be useful for local Christian communities.

Purpose of the Programme

The following pastoral programme is primarily designed for animation in local Christian communities. While a variety of action-research projects exist at national and regional levels, local Christian communities must provide a base for education and action on the problems of justice in Canada and the Third World. It is important, therefore, that more attention and resources be given to the task of developing projects in local communities.

The basic purpose of this pastoral programme is to stimulate people in local Christian communities to:

(a) develop a critical awareness of the realities and structures of injustice in both Canada and the Third World;

(b) act in solidarity with poor and oppressed peoples engaged in struggles for justice and liberation;

(c) reflect on these experiences in the light of the Gospel and the social teachings of the Church.

Working Instruments

To facilitate the development of pastoral programmes in local Christian communities, two working instruments have been prepared: one on Justice in Canada; the other on Justice in the Third World. These working instruments are designed as resource guides for local animators. They are not meant to be used for direct animation. Instead, they have been designed primarily to assist animators in developing their own projects for study and action in local Christian communities. The two working instruments contain separate sections on a variety of issues, each of which provides: (a) a brief analysis of the issue; (b) a list of resource materials that may be used for study and/or animation; (c) a brief set of notes on some Christian groups engaged in action on the issue; (d) some questions for reflection on the part of the animators.

Justice in Canada

The working instrument on Justice in Canada is designed to stimulate some critical awareness and action on various social and economic realities of injustice in the context of the Canadian paradox. This working instrument takes up the topics of (i) the economic order and (ii) the political order of this country and goes on to focus attention on problems of social and economic injustices: (iii) continuing poverty; (iv) industrial exploitation; (v) production and needs; (vi) regional development; (vii) community development; (viii) northern development; (ix) consumer society; (x) minority discrimination; (xi) social control.

This outline of topics, issues, and resource materials is not meant to be comprehensive. Moreover, the working instrument itself requires further completion and refinement by the animators themselves.

Justice in the Third World

The working instrument on Justice in the Third World is designed to stimulate some critical awareness and action on injustices in the Third World in the context of the Canadian paradox. This chapter is divided into ten sections dealing with the following topics: (i) underdevelopment of the Third World; (ii) the global economy; (iii) self-reliant development; (iv) foreign aid; (v) international trade; (vi) foreign investment; (vii) world hunger; (viii) repression of human rights; (ix) military armament; and (x) immigration. Once again, the topics and resource materials are not meant to be comprehensive and the working instrument itself requires further completion and refinement by animators themselves.

Places for Animation

... education demands a renewal of heart, a renewal based on the recognition of sin in its individual and social manifestations.

... It will likewise awaken a critical sense which will lead us to reflect on the society in which we live and on its values;

... the principal aim of this education is to awaken consciousness to a knowledge of the concrete situation.

... it is also practical education: it comes through action, participation and vital contact with the reality of injustice.
(Justice in the World, *No. 51, 53*)

In the life of the Church itself, there are many different types of local Christian communities. Yet, for most of these communities, little attention has been given to the pastoral task of developing critical awareness, action, and reflection on the problems of justice. It should be noted that there are both problems and possibilities to be found in developing effective programmes for education and action in the various types of communities. A great deal depends on the people involved and the style of animation employed. In various dioceses, local Social Action groups and Development and Peace committees may find those working instruments useful in their regular programmes. At the same time, there are several other important places for animation which could make use of the working instruments:

Parish Communities:

(The local parish continues to be a central place for Christian activities and should provide opportunities for education and action on issues of justice).

Religious Communities:

(In reviewing their vocations, more religious communities could focus their pastoral work on the struggles of the poor and the oppressed).

School Programmes:

> (The curriculum of local schools could include courses designed to increase the critical awareness of young people about the problems of justice).

Seminary Programmes:

> (Education for justice should be a major part of the seminary curriculum in training people for the priesthood and religious life).

Family Projects:

> (The family is an important place for nurturing Christian values and education for justice should be part of family life).

Ecumenical Groups:

> (Activities for justice often provide the occasion for Christians of different denominational backgrounds to express their common faith).

Lay Organizations:

> (There are a variety of lay organizations in the Church which could participate in education and action projects for justice).

Community Groups:

> (Local community organizations have often been important places where Christians have been involved in education and action projects for social and economic justice).

Popular Groups

In order to deepen and strengthen one's Christian commitment to justice, it is important to become involved in the specific struggles of popular groups. All around us here in Canada, as of course in the Third World, there are a variety of popular groups — exploited workers, poor peoples' groups, tenants' unions, Native people, the jobless, small farmers, small fishermen, refugees, cultural minorities, racial minorities — and many more who are directly involved in struggles to defend their basic human rights. By acting in solidarity with these groups, Christians are better able to identify the problems of injustice and participate more effectively in the transformation of society.

It should be noted that the various types of Christian communities and popular groups are not equipped with the same resources necessary for community action. It is up to the animator to identify the needs and resources of his or her group and to utilize the working instruments for the purpose of analyzing, acting and reflecting on specific problems of social and economic injustice.

Elements of Animation

"... Our basic principle must be: only knowledge gained through participation is valid in this area of justice; true knowledge can be gained only through concern and solidarity. We must have recourse to the biblical notion of knowledge, experience shared with others. We have too frequently separated evangelization from social action, and reserved social involvement to elites and, eventually, to the clergy. Unless we are in solidarity with the people who are poor, marginal, or isolated we cannot even speak effectively about their problems.

Theoretical knowledge is indispensable, but it is partial and limited; when it abstracts from lived concrete experience, it merely projects the present into the future."
(Cardinal Flahiff, **Christian Formation for Justice**, 1971)

There are, of course, many different kinds of pedagogies and technical skills that may be used in education for justice. Yet, experience has shown that critical awareness for the sake of transforming society cannot be effectively stimulated by lectures, or lessons, or sermons alone. Effective animation requires a process of action and reflection on the demands for justice. For people develop a critical awareness primarily through direct participation in social struggles on specific issues of injustice. The two working instruments themselves are primarily designed to be used for this kind of animation.

Action and Reflection

The praxis of action and reflection on specific issues of injustice provides people with an occasion for developing critical awareness for the sake of transforming society. Action and reflection are two inseparable parts of the process. To engage in action without reflection leads to forms of activism and runs the risk of becoming less critical and more naive both in terms of understanding the social structures that cause human suffering and the theological importance of acting on the issue. On the other hand, thinking and talking about injustices without participation in concrete action leads to forms of intellectualism and runs the risk of developing knowledge that is not oriented towards the transformation of society.

Christian Action Approaches

Over the past several decades, some Christian communities have followed the working methodology developed in the Catholic action movement. This entails a three-fold discipline: (1) **Observe:** identifying the injustices in a particular situation; (2) **Judge:** making some moral judgments about the injustice for the sake of action in the light of the Gospel; (3) **Act:** taking some specific actions to deal with the particular problem of injustice. In recent years, Christian communities have further developed and refined this methodology, emphasizing the importance of: working directly with popular groups; developing a deeper analysis of the structural causes of injustice; identifying the common links that exist between various social struggles; and reflecting theologically on specific action experiences.

Social Analysis

Social analysis is an important part of reflecting on specific action experiences for justice. This entails a scientific analysis of the economic, political, and social structures that cause human suffering and injustices in particular situations. Wherever possible, this kind of social analysis should be carried out in dialogue with the popular groups engaged in the particular social struggle. In this way, the people participating in specific action for justice can develop a common analysis of the structures that cause injustice for the sake of future action.

Theological Reflection

Theological reflection is an essential part of reflecting on specific action experiences for justice. The Scriptures and the social teachings of the Church provide critical insights for making value judgments about particular situations of injustice and for reflecting on the deeper spiritual meeting of justice and liberation in the light of God's plan for salvation. Again, wherever possible, this kind of theological reflection should be carried out in dialogue with the popular groups engaged in the specific action. In this way, the various people involved in specific activities for justice can deepen their knowledge of God and strengthen their faith in Christ.

Common Links

The common links or connections that exist between different social struggles within our society and between Canada and the Third World are also an important part of reflecting on actions for justice. For example, participation in the struggles against apartheid in South Africa can stimulate critical awareness and action on racism experienced by people here in our society. The reverse is also true. Moreover, active participation and reflection on the problems of injustice in one region of Canada can lead to a greater awareness of similar problems and causes of injustice in another region. Thus, common links which authentically exist between different social struggles can help to further develop critical awareness for the sake of transforming society.

Some References:

Paul VI, **Octogesima Adveniens,** Apostolic letter to Cardinal Maurice Roy, Vatican City, 1971.

Pope Paul VI's letter urging Christian communities to become involved in analyzing and transforming society from the standpoint of Gospel values. Full text available in **Gospel of Peace and Justice** (Orbis Books, Maryknoll, New York. 1976).

Canadian Bishops, **A Society to Be Transformed,** Canadian Conference of Catholic Bishops, 1977.

A major statement of the Canadian bishops urging Christian communities to take a critical look at our social and economic system from the standpoint of the Gospel message of love and justice. Available at cost on order from the Publication Service, Canadian Conference of Catholic Bishops, 90 Parent Avenue, Ottawa, Ontario, K1N 7B1.

Fenton, T., **Education for Justice,** Orbis Books, Maryknoll, New York, 1975, 464 pages.

An important resource manual particularly for developing education programmes in schools and universities. Includes a variety of educational designs for developing critical awareness about the realities and causes of injustice. Also includes several models of course studies along with resource lists and background readings. Available on order from your local bookstore.

Freire, P., **Pedagogy of the Oppressed,** Herder and Herder, New York, 1971, 186 pages.

A major statement on the pedagogy of action and reflection. Available on order from your local bookstore.

Grand' Maison, J., **Pour une pédagogie sociale d'auto-développement en éducation,** Stanké, Montréal, 1976, 191 pages.

Présentation d'une approche pédagogique globale visant la recréation d'une base sociale plus dynamique et plus solidaire dans les institutions et dans les collectivités régionales et locales. Disponible en librairie.

Segundo, L., **The Liberation of Theology,** Orbis Books, Maryknoll, New York, 1976.

An analysis of theological method emphasizing the dialectical relationship between theory and praxis, with a firm grounding in social analysis of the concrete situation. Available on order from your local bookstore or library.

Additional Resources

In addition to the resource materials identified in the text above, there are a variety of other resource tools that may be useful for Christian animators.

1. Audio-Visual on Canadian Social Teachings:

The Canadian Religious Conference, Development and Peace, and other Catholic organizations have prepared slide-tape presentations based on the social messages of the Canadian bishops.

—**Sharing Daily Bread,** (based on the 1974 Labour Day Message of the Canadian Bishops.)

—**Northern Development: At What Cost?** (based on the 1975 Labour Day message of the Canadian Bishops.)

—**From Words to Action** (based on the 1976 Labour Day message of the Canadian Bishops.)

—**A Society to be Transformed** (based on the 1977 Social Message of the Canadian Bishops.)

Copies are available on order from Kevin Moynahan Studios, Suite 330, 144 Front Street West, Toronto, Ontario, M5J 1G2.

2. Justice and Peace Documents:

The Pontifical Commission for Justice and Peace has prepared several documents relating the Church's official social teachings to several topics. The following are some examples which are available on order from your local Catholic bookstore.

—Land, P., **An Overview,** Vatican City, 1972. (An overview of the Synod of Bishops on Justice in the World.)

—Ward, B., **A New Creation? Environmental Issues,** Vatican City, 1972. (A follow-up paper to the Synod on Justice in the World).

—**Holy See and Disarmament,** Vatican City, 1975. (Draws together basic papal teaching on peace and the global arms race.)

—**Self-Reliance,** Vatican City, 1978. (Prepared for the Third Development Decade of the United Nations.)

—**Universal Purpose of Created Things,** Vatican City, 1977. (Prepared for the United Nations Conference on the Law of the Sea.)

3. History of Christian Social Action

Various historical studies have been done on the history of Christian social action in Canada. The following examples are available on order from your local bookstore or library.

—Allen, R., **The Social Passion,** University of Toronto Press, Toronto, 1971. (A history of the social gospel movement in western Canada, 1918-1928.)

—Dumont, F., et alii, **Histoire de l'action catholique au Canada français,** Montréal, Editions Fides, 1971. (Une étude effectuée dans le cadre d'un projet de recherche sur l'histoire de l'Eglise québécoise. L'étude porte sur le développement du mouvement des travailleurs catholiques, du mouvement coopératif et autres expériences d'action sociale.)

—Laidlaw, A., **The Man from Margaree,** McClelland and Stewart, Toronto, 1971. (The writings and speeches of Moses Coady pertaining to the Antigonish Movement in the Maritimes.)

4. Social Ethics

Various people working in the field of ethical and social analysis have focused attention on struggles for justice and the development of peoples. The following are some examples available on order from your local bookstore or library.

—Baum, G., **The Social Imperative,** Paulist Press, New York, 1979. (Includes the theological reflection on some social and political realities in Canada.)

—Goulet, D., **A New Moral Order: Development Ethics and Liberation Theology,** Orbis Books, Maryknoll, New York. 1974. (Explores relations between ethical thought and liberation theology.)

—Goulet, D., **The Cruel Choice: A New Concept in the Theory of Development,** Atheneum, New York, 1971. (An ethical study of the economic and social aspects of development).

—Grand' Maison, J., **Nouveaux modèles sociaux et développement,** Hurtubise, Montréal, HMH, 1972. (L'auteur examine la relation entre les nouveaux modèles de société et le développement des peuples.)

—Grand' Maison, J., **Une société en quête d'éthique,** Editions Fides, Montréal, 1977. (Cahiers de recherche éthique, no 5.)

—Kerans, P., **Sinful Social Structures,** Paulist Press, New York, 1974. (An ethical critique of western capitalism and technological society.)

—Manarouche, A., **Y a-t-il une éthique sociale chrétienne?** Seuil, Paris, 1969. (Les questions qui sont impliquées dans l'élaboration d'une éthique chrétienne contemporaine.)

5. Theology and Liberation

In addition to the publications identified earlier in this working paper, there are several other examples of theological reflection on social struggles for justice and liberation.

—Alves, R.A., **Christianisme, opium ou libération?** les Editions du Cerf, Paris, 1972. (Une étude sur la théologie de l'espoir humain et la libération humaine.)

—Laurentin, R., **Nouvelles dimensions de l'espérance,** les Editions du Cerf, Paris, 1972. (Une étude sur la théologie de l'espoir et la libération.)

—Lockhead, D., **The Liberation of the Bible,** Student Christian Movement, Toronto, 1977. (Explores the problem of intepreting the Scriptures from an ideological standpoint and discusses methods for biblical reflections. Available on order from the Student Christian Movement, 736 Bathurst Street, Toronto 4, Ontario.)

—Moltmann, J., **Gospel of Liberation,** Orbis Books, Maryknoll, New York, 1973. (A theological analysis of the basic liberation themes in the Gospel.)

—Segundo, J., **Theology and the Artisans of a New Humanity,** five volume study, Orbis Books, Maryknoll, New York, 1968 and 1972. (An integration of the liberation motif with the major treatises of classical theology. Based on experiences of dialogue with a reflection group in Montevideo.)

—Reuther, R., **The Radical Kingdom,** Paulist Press, New York, 1972. (An example of liberation theology by a theologian engaged in reflection on the women's movement.)

—**The Challenge of Black Theology in South Africa,** Orbis Books, Maryknoll, New York, 1974. (A collection of essays on liberation theology in the context of South Africa.)

6. Christology and Liberation:

The life of Jesus Christ, His concern for the poor and the oppressed and His message for the salvation of mankind, have been the subject of numerous books, articles, and statements. The following examples are available on order from your local bookstore or library.

—Boff, L. **Jésus-Christ Libérateur,** les Editions du Cerf, Paris, 1974. (Présentation de Jésus dans le cadre de la théologie de la libération.)

—Conseil permanent de l'Episcopat français, **Libérations humaines et salut en Jésus-Christ,** Le Centurion, Paris, 1975, 108 pages. (Une réflexion sur les relations entre les luttes de libération et le salut en Jésus-Christ.)

—Massalski, C., **Le Christ, libération de l'homme d'aujourd'hui, les Editions du Fayard, Paris, 1975.** (Comment Jésus-Christ répond aux problèmes fondamentaux de l'homme d'aujourd'hui.)

—Sobrino, J., **Christology at the Crossroads,** Orbis Books, Maryknoll, New York, 1978. (One of the more recent studies on Christology from the standpoint of liberation theology in Latin America.)

7. Ecclesiology and Liberation/Development:

The new and emerging role of the Church and Christian communities in the liberation and development of peoples has been explored in several studies. The following examples are available on order from your local bookstore or library.

—Bigo, P., **The Church and Third World Revolution,** Orbis Books, Maryknoll, New York, 1977. (Discusses the role of the Church in response to the demands for justice in the Third World.)

—Cussianovich, A., **Religious Life and the Poor,** Orbis Books, Maryknoll, New York, 1979. (A reappraisal of the meaning of religious life in the light of the liberation theology.)

—Ellacuria, L., **Freedom Made Flesh,** Orbis Books, Maryknoll, New York, 1976. (Explores the role of the Church in announcing and building the Kingdom of God in history.)

—Messier, M., **Foi et développement,** Bellarmin, Montréal, 1974. (Une étude de la relation entre la foi et le développement.)

—Neal, M. Sr., **A Socio-Theology of Letting Go,** Paulist Press, New York, 1977. (Discusses new forms of involvement by Christian communities in social justice and theological reflection.)

—Segundo, J., **The Community Called Church,** Orbis Books, Maryknoll, New York, 1973. (Explores some major questions about new forms of Christian communities in relation to the Gospel of justice and liberation.)

—Segundo, J., **Catéchisme pour aujourd'hui,** trois volumes, les Editions du Cerf, Paris, 1972. (Une étude sur trois sujets: chercher Dieu, recréer l'Eglise, voir la liberté.)

8. Liturgy and Social Justice:

The relationship between the liturgy and action for justice has been explored in several ways. The following examples are available from your local bookstore or library.

—de Margerie, B., **The Sacraments and Social Progess,** Franciscan Herald Press, Chicago, 1974. (Discusses the meaning of the sacraments in relation to ethical themes pertaining to the development of peoples.)

—Dugrive et Guichard, **Politique et vocabulaire liturgique,** Seuil, Paris, 1978. (Etude sur les implications politiques du langage liturgique.)

—Hamman, A., **Vie liturgique et vie sociale,** Desclée de Brouwer, Paris, 1968. (Une étude des relations historiques entre l'eucharistie et la justice sociale.)

9. Prayer and Social Justice

The question of spirituality, or the relationship between prayer and action, has been explored in several recent publications. The following examples are available on order from your local bookstore or library.

—Canadian bishops, **Fulness of Life,** Pastoral Message, Pentecost, 1978. (Outlines some basic elements of a Christian spirituality.)

—Christenson, L., **A Charismatic Approach to Social Action,** Lakeland Press, London, 1975. (A look at how prayer and action may be related in the pursuit of social justice.)

—Fahey, S., **Charismatic Social Action:** Reflection Resource Manual, Paulist Press, Paremus, 1977. (A guide to resources on the relationship between spirituality and social action.)

—Guetny, Besuard et al. **Prière et vie selon la foi,** les Editions ouvrières, Paris, 1976. (Etude sur la prière, l'action et la lutte pour la justice.)

10. Faith and Political Action

The relationship between Christian faith and political action is explored in a variety of ways by different publications. The following examples are available from your local bookstore or library.

—Ancel, A., **Pour une lecture chrétienne de la lutte des classes,** Editions universitaires, Paris, 1975. (Un ouvrage qui vise à aider les chrétiens à mieux découvrir le Christ dans leur action quotidienne.)

—Aubert, J.M., **Vivre en chrétien au xxe siècle,** tome 2, Salvator, 1977. (Etude sur les fondements théologiques de l'engagement chrétien.)

Centre de pastorale en milieu ouvrier, **La politique et l'Evangile,** dossiers "vie ouvrière", no 96, 1975. (Une série de brefs articles sur l'Evangile, la foi et l'action politique. Disponible en écrivant à CPMO, 1201 rue Visitation, Montréal., P.Q., H2L 3B5.)

—Coste, R., **Les chrétiens et la lutte des classes,** S.O.S., Paris, 1975. (Une étude sur la relation entre la foi chrétienne et la lutte des classes.)

—Girardi, G., **Chrétiens pour le socialisme,** les Editions du Cerf, Paris, 1976. (Les questions réciproques que se posent chrétiens et socialistes.)

—Gonzales-Ruiz, J.M., **The New Creation: Marxist and Christian?** Orbis Books, 1976. (Explores relationship between Christianity and Marxism.)

—Petulla, J., **Christian Political Theology,** Orbis Books, Maryknoll, New York, 1976. (A Marxist perspective on Christian political theology.)

Some Relevant Periodicals

In addition to the books listed above, there are a variety of periodicals which often publish articles on the relationship between church and society, theology and social issues, religion and politics. The following are some examples of such periodicals in Canada.

Chelsea Journal: A bi-monthly Canadian periodical that takes up literary, religious and political views in relation to current social issues. Available on order from the Chelsea Journal, 1437 College Drive, Saskatoon, Sask., S7N 0W6.

L'Eglise canadienne: Revue bimensuelle de documentation et d'information sur la pensée et l'activité de l'Eglise au Canada. Disponible en s'adressant à: l'Eglise canadienne, 1073, boul. St-Cyrille ouest, Québec, G1S 4R5.

Nouveau dialogue: Revue publiée par le Service Incroyance et Foi (cinq numéros par année), incluant à l'occasion des articles sur le dialogue entre chrétiens et marxistes. Disponible en s'adressant à: Service Incroyance et Foi, 2930 rue Lacombe, Montréal, H3T 1G4.

Relations: Publication mensuelle sous la responsabilité d'un groupe de membres de la Compagnie de Jésus sur des questions théologiques et sociales. Disponible en écrivant à: Relations, 8100 Boul. St-Laurent, Montréal, H2P 2G9.

The Ecumenist: A bi-monthly publication which often includes articles on theological and social questions. Available on order from the Ecumenist, 545 Island Road, Ramsey, New Jersey, 07446.

The following are examples of other relevant periodicals published elsewhere.

—**America:** A weekly publication of the Jesuits that often includes articles on theology and current social issues. Available on order from America, 106 West 56th Street, New York, New York, 10019.

—**Cahiers de l'actualité religieuse et sociale:** Publication bimensuelle qui dégage les éléments favorisant des choix responsables dans l'Eglise et dans la vie socio-politique. Disponible en écrivant à: Cahiers de l'actualité religieuse et sociale, 14 rue d'Assas, 75006, Paris, France.

—**Christian Century:** A weekly periodical that often features articles on the Church, theology and current social issues. Available on order from the Christian Century, 407 S. Dearborn St., Chicago, Illinois, 60605.

—**Church Alert:** An ecumenical periodical on global social issues, published quarterly by SODEPAX, a joint committee of the Pontifical Commission for Justice and Peace and the Justice and Service division of the World Council of Churches. Available on order from SODEPAX, Ecumenical Center, P.O.B. 66, 150 Route de Ferney, 1211 Geneva 20, Switzerland.

—**Commonweal:** A weekly periodical that often includes articles on Church and society. Available on order from Commonweal, 232 Madison Avenue, New York, New York, 10016.

—**Cross Currents:** A quarterly publication which often features articles on major theological and social issues. Available on order from Cross Currents, Mercy College, Dobbs Ferry, New York, 10522.

Project Feedback

Project Feedback was a cross-country survey of people's attitudes in the Canadian Church, sponsored by the Canadian Conference of Canadian Bishops. Conducted by G. Maxwell, this survey involved person-to-person conversations with some 750 people in 40 urban and rural communities across Canada in 1974 and 1975. The results of the survey were reported in five installments: (1) People's Social Hopes; (2) Assessing Daily Life; (3) Searching for Wholeness; (4) What's Expected of Religious Leadership; (5) How People Feel About the 1980s. Copies of a **Resumé** of these reports are available at cost from the Publication Service, the Canadian Conference of Catholic Bishops, 90 Parent Avenue, Ottawa, Ontario, K1N 7B1.

JUSTICE
IN
CANADA

Introduction

In Canada, various parts of the Christian community have been developing a critical awareness of the problems of justice facing our society today. Through a series of annual Labour Day messages and pastoral statements, for example, the Canadian bishops have been engaged in a process of analyzing and commenting on a wide range of social and economic issues from the standpoint of Gospel values. At the same time, a variety of Christian groups and action-research projects throughout the country have been developing a more in-depth analysis of specific social issues and structures of injustice.

This chapter is a working paper for Christian animators concerned about the problems of social and economic justice in Canada. It is designed to stimulate a more critical awareness of the problems and causes of underdevelopment in our society. The objectives are four-fold: (i) to briefly identify and comment on some of the basic problems and structures of injustice in our society; (ii) to list some resource materials which may be useful for study and animation; (iii) to identify some Christian education and action programmes on specific issues; (iv) to pose some questions for reflection on the part of Christian animators.

The central theme of this working paper concerns one side of the "double paradox". On the one hand, Canada is considered to be a "developed" country, enjoying the wealth, liberties and comforts of a modern industrialized society. On the other hand, this country bears the marks of an underdeveloped society: continuing poverty, class divisions, regional disparities, foreign control, economic dependency and a variety of related problems. Indeed, we have been called the "richest underdeveloped country" in the world. This is the paradox that underlies our discussion in this chapter concerning the problems and structures of injustice in Canada as a modern capitalist country.

In Canada today, this paradox is present in the different societies and regions that make up this country. There are, for example, some distinctions to be made between the experience of Québecois society and the rest of Canadian society in terms of economic, cultural, social and political realities. This working paper tries to be aware of some of these distinctions. Taken together however, the various societies and regions that comprise Canada today dramatize the social and economic injustices that lie at the center of this paradox.

The working paper is divided into eleven sections dealing with various topics. The first two sections identify some of the basic structural problems in our economic and political order. The other nine sections focus on specific issues of social and economic injustices: Continuing Poverty, Industrial Exploitation, Production and Needs, Regional Development, Community Development, Northern Development, Consumer Society, Minority Discrimination, Social Control. Each of these topics illustrates different aspects of the paradox. Yet, each section may be treated as a separate unit for study and reflection by animators, recognizing that there are internal relationships between the various parts and the topics themselves.

There are, however, several limitations to be noted concerning the use of this working paper. First, the various topics taken up are not the only examples of injustice in our society. Indeed, this working paper tends to focus more on the problems of justice in our socio-economic order. Secondly, the list of resource materials is neither comprehensive nor complete. Most of the resource materials have been selected because they are helpful in stimulating a more critical awareness of injustices in our society. There may, indeed, be contradictions in the various analytical viewpoints put forward in the resource materials. It is, therefore, important to recognize that these resource materials do not necessarily represent the position or policy of the bishops on the various topics under discussion. They are presented for the information of animators.*

*The resource materials are listed in alphabetical order. Those resource materials which may be useful for animation purposes are identified by (A) and those which are more useful for study purposes are identified by (S).

Finally, it should be understood that this is a "working" instrument for animators. For this very reason, this document is incomplete. It proposes a framework for Christians to develop critical awareness and action concerning the problems and structures of injustice in our society. Yet, this framework requires further refinement and development by animators directly engaged in education and action on these and related local issues of injustice. The set of questions proposed at the end of several sections may help to facilitate some reflections for these purposes.

General References

It is, of course, impossible to identify all the relevant data and resource materials pertaining to specific issues of Justice in Canada. In addition to the more specific references listed in this working paper, there are some general references that may be useful for animators.

a) There are some publications that provide current data and identify resource materials useful for analyzing social and economic problems in Canada.

—**Connexions:** A bilingual publication that provides both a brief summary of resource materials on various socio-economic issues and information on Christian groups and others engaged in the transformation of society. For further information, contact Connexions, 121 Avenue Road, Toronto, Ontario, M5R 2G3.

—**Synthesis:** A monthly publication that surveys major newspapers in Canada, analyzing and synthesizing current economic, political, cultural and social issues. For further information, contact the Canadian News Synthesis Project, Box 6300, Station "A", Toronto, Ontario, M5W 1P7.

b) **Audio-Visual Catalogues:** A variety of films and slide-tape shows useful for animation purposes are available from several sources.

—The Development Education Centre has a library of films and slide tape presentations pertaining to social, economic and cultural issues in Canada. For the DEC catalogue, contact the Development Education Centre, 121 Avenue Road, Toronto, Ontario, M5R 2G3.

—The National Film Board library contains a wide range of films, some of which are useful for animation purposes. For the NFB catalogue, contact the National Film Board, 150 Kent Street, Ottawa, Ontario.

c) **Diocesan Projects:** Some dioceses have designed their own study-action projects and resource materials concerning problems of injustice for example:

—the Archdiocese of Toronto has developed a series of pilot projects in social ministry in several parishes. For further information contact the Social Action Office, Archdiocese of Toronto, Suite 101, 12 Shuter, Toronto, Ontario M5B 1A2.

—the Archdiocese of Québec has developed an ongoing programme of social information and awareness. For further information, contact l'Office de la pastorale sociale, 1073, boulevard Saint-Cyrille ouest, Québec G1S 4R5.

1. Economic Order

Many people agree that there is something wrong with the present social and economic order. It fails to serve the human needs of the majority of people. The present economic order results in the very uneven distribution of wealth and the control of resources by a small minority.
*(Canadian Bishops, **From Words to Action,** 1976)*

Although our country is called developed, it has marks of underdevelopment. In 1971, one person in four had an income below the poverty level. Since then inflation and high unemployment rates have worsened the situation. Powerful foreign-controlled companies exercise increasing power in society beyond the reach of effective public intervention. Their decisions directly influence housing, unemployment, increasing prices and the declining values of earnings and savings. Economic and social disparities between regions of the country persist. Pollution and other forms of environmental damage show that natural resources are misused. Entire groups who are central to our country's future are uncertain of the survival of their very culture and customs. Workers, even those in unions, have little share in decisions affecting their livelihood and well-being. In turn, elected representatives at various levels of government seem to face insurmountable difficulties.
*(Canadian Bishops, **A Society to be Transformed,** 1977)*

In the eyes of most people, Canada is a "developed" society, enjoying the wealth and comforts of an industrialized country. A closer look, however, reveals that this society bears many of the marks of "underdevelopment". While Canada is not a Third World country, it does have some of the basic problems that characterize underdeveloped nations: continuing poverty, social inequalities, regional disparities, foreign control, economic dependency, minority discrimination, etc. Indeed, our economic order has been built in such a way as to serve the interests of a small minority rather than to serve the basic needs of all people in this country. Today, economic power is concentrated in the hands of a small number of powerful corporations, many of which are foreign-owned. The decisions of these corporations have a profound impact in shaping our economic order and determining the patterns of development and underdevelopment in our society. The following are some of the basic characteristics of our economic order.

Global Economy

Like many countries, Canada's economic order has been largely shaped by its role in the global economy itself. Historically, Canada first entered the global economy as a colony of France and later Britain. Over the span of some three centuries, the colonies of Canada were populated and organized to supply France and later Britain with such resources as furs, fish, lumber and wheat. Thus, Canada's economy was originally organized to supply resources and provide markets for colonial powers. While Canada has since been gradually transformed into an industrialized society, this country still serves as a resource hinterland for larger industrialized powers. Today, the Canadian economy is largely organized to serve the interests of the United States (and to a lesser extent Japan and Western Europe), supplying natural resources for their industries and providing markets for the sale of their products. Indeed, through complex trade patterns and the operations of large corporations, Canada has become locked into a continental economy dominated by the United States.

(S) Fréchette, P., et alii, **L'économie du Québec,** les Editions HRW, Montréal, 1975, 436 pages.

Un ouvrage sur l'économie québécoise contemporaine, ses forces et ses faiblesses. Disponible en librairie.

(S) Gonick, C., **Inflation or Depression:** An analysis of the Continuing Crisis of the Canadian Economy, James Lorimer and Co., Toronto, 1975, 440 pages.

An analysis of some of the basic structural problems in Canada's economy. Available on order from your local bookstore or library.

(S) Levitt, Kari, **Silent Surrender,** MacMillan of Canada, Toronto, 1970, 185 pages.

A major study on the foreign control of Canada's economy. Available on order from your local bookstore.

(S) Quaden, G., **Le néo-capitalisme. Une économie politique du capitalisme contemporain,** Ed. Jean-Pierre Delarge, Paris, 1976.

Un ouvrage-synthèse sur les réalités économiques du monde contemporain. Facilement abordable, cet ouvrage comprend une bibliographie qui complète chacun des chapitres.

Transnational Corporations

Since the second world war, the transnational corporation has emerged as the dominant force that is shaping our economy and that of other countries. The guiding principles of these corporations are expanding growth and the accumulation of wealth. Within the global economy, it is imperative for transnational companies to gain control over supplies of natural resources and markets for the sale of their products, in order to guarantee rising profit margins. In several cases today, transnational corporations wield more economic power than nation states themselves. And, in this country, the transnationals have had an enormous impact on the social, economic, political, and cultural lives of peoples and society. Yet, they are accountable and responsible only to themselves.

(S) Barnet, R., and Muller, R., **Global Reach,** Simon and Schuster, New York, 1974, 508 pages.

The most complete study of the power and influence of transnational corporations to date. Available on order from your local bookstore.

(S) Sabatier, A., **Les sociétés multinationales,** Paris, Le Centurion, 1975, 169 pages.

Une série de questions et réponses relatives aux multinationales. Disponible en librairie.

(S) Sabatier, A., Dubly, M., **Dossier Multinationales,** Paris, Tema Editions, 1974, 127 pages.

Un ensemble de données sur quelques-unes des plus importantes multinationales. Disponible en bibliothèque.

(S) Vernon, R., **Les entreprises multinationales; la souveraineté des Etats en péril,** Calman-Levy, Paris, 1973, 345 pages.

Un classique sur le pouvoir des multinationales face à l'Etat. Disponible en librairie.

(A) **Who's In Control?** Issue No. 14, United Church of Canada Publication, Toronto, January 1977, 8 pages.

A popular introduction to corporations and their influence in our society. Available by writing to the United Church of Canada, 85 St Clair Avenue East, Toronto, Ontario.

Foreign Ownership

Almost 65% of Canada's economy is estimated to be controlled by foreign-owned corporations. Indeed, foreign-owned corporations control several key sectors of Canada's economy: 58% of manufacturing; 65% of mining; 74% of oil and gas; 99% of petroleum refining; 96% of automotive industry; 79% of electrical apparatus. A large percentage of these corporations are based in the United States. Through direct investment, American-based corporations have established branch plants in Canada, thereby securing ownership and control over key sectors of the Canadian economy, notably in manufacturing and resource industries. As a result, our economy is primarily geared to serve the interests of these foreign-owned corporations rather than the development needs of people in Canada.

(S) Gordon, W., **Storm Signals,** McClelland and Stewart, Toronto, 1975, 140 pages.

An analysis of foreign ownership in relation to Canada's current economic problems. Available on order from your local bookstore or library.

(S) Government of Canada, **Foreign Direct Investments in Canada,** Information Canada, Ottawa, 1972.

The official government study on foreign investment in Canada. Available on order from your local bookstore.

(S) Gouvernement du Québec, Conseil exécutif, **Le cadre et les moyens d'une politique québécoise concernant les investissements étrangers: rapport du Comité interministériel sur les investissements étrangers,** Editeur officiel, Québec, 1973, (texte révisé de mars à juin 1974), 203 pages.

Une analyse du rôle des investissements étrangers dans l'économie québécoise. Disponible en bibliothèque.

(S) Raynauld, A., **La propriété des entreprises au Québec,** Les presses de l'Université de Montréal, Montréal, 1974.

Une étude sur la propriété réelle des entreprises oeuvrant au Québec. Disponible en librairie.

Economic Dependency

In effect, Canada's economy has become highly dependent upon the United States and other industrialized countries for the capital and technology required for economic development and for the products and goods necessary for daily life. Rather than using the capital from earnings and savings of Canadians to finance economic development in Canada, our major banks have traditionally reinvested large portions of this money elsewhere, making Canada increasingly dependent on foreign capital and technology. Instead of developing our own natural resources — minerals, timber, oil, gas, water — to serve the long-term development needs of people in this country, many of our most valuable resources are exported to other countries where they are manufactured into finished products and sold back to us at much higher prices. Yet once Canada's wealth-generating, non-renewable resources are exhausted, our economy will be left in a fragile and vulnerable state, unable to serve adequately the needs of our population.

(S) Bourgeault, P., **Structure of Canadian Industry,** Science Council of Canada, Study No. 23, 1973, 135 pages.

A critical review of Canada's resource and manufacturing policies. Available on order from your local bookstore.

(S) Cordell, A., **Foreign Direct Investment and Canadian Science Policy,** Science Council of Canada, Background Study No. 22, 1971, Ottawa.

A somewhat technical review of Canada's dependence upon foreign capital and technology. Available on order from your local bookstore.

Concentration of Corporate Power

In Canada, economic power has been concentrated in the hands of a small number of large corporations. In a recent study, Statistics Canada concluded that out of 30,000 companies studied only 100 account for 46% of all business activity in this country. Moreover, on the basis of the 1974 tax returns, it has been shown that 46% of profits were recorded by the 311 largest Canadian corporations, slightly more than one tenth of one percent of all companies that filed tax returns that year. At the same time, a small number of large corporations effectively control business activity in several of Canada's key industries. Free enterprise and free markets have become a disappearing phenomenon. By restricting production, large corporations are able to determine market prices. By lowering prices, they can effectively force small business and small producers out of the market.

(S) Clement, W., **The Canadian Corporate Elite,** Carleton Library No. 89, McClelland and Stewart, 1975, 479 pages.

An analysis of the concentration of corporate power in Canada. Available on order from your local bookstore.

(S) Fournier, P., **The Québec Establishment,** Black Rose Books, Montréal, 1976, 228 pages.

A study that deals with the concentration of corporate power in Quebec. Available on order from your local bookstore.

(S) Sales, A., (dir), **Les industriels au Québec et leur rôle dans le développement économique,** rapport intermédiaire présenté au Ministère de l'industrie et du commerce du Québec par le groupe de recherche sur les élites industrielles au Québec, Montréal, 252 pages.

Role of the State

Federal and provincial governments have traditionally played a major role in creating favourable conditions for the accumulation of wealth by corporations. In playing this role, governments have performed several functions: designing fiscal and monetary policies to stimulate economic growth for private business; underwriting the risks of private production by using public funds to provide subsidies, grants, tax incentives and financial guarantees for industrial projects; undertaking the construction of technical infrastructures such as roads, highways, railways, bridges, harbours, and other facilities as a pre-condition for industrial projects; regulating the supply of labour through manpower and immigration policies; absorbing the social costs of industrial development through the provision of sanitation services, medicare, unemployment insurance, education facilities.

(S) Chodos, R., **The CPR: A Century of Corporate Welfare,** James Lewis and Samuel Publishers, Toronto, 1973, 152 pages.

A case study showing how public subsidies have facilitated the expanding wealth and power of the CPR. Available on order from your local library.

(S) Dosman, E., **The National Interest: The Politics of Northern Development, 1968-75,** McClelland and Stewart, Toronto, 1975, 209 pages.

A case study showing how federal government policies on northern development have been largely geared to serve the interests of the major petroleum companies. Available on order from your local bookstore or library.

(S) Fournier, P., **Les sociétés d'Etat et les objectifs économiques,** OPDQ, Editeur officiel, Québec, 1977.

Une étude consacrée au rôle du gouvernement et plus particulièrement celui des sociétes d'Etat dans la vie économique québécoise.
Disponible en bibliothèque.

(S)   Fréchette, P., et alii, **l'Economie du Québec,** les Editions HRW, Montréal, 1975, 346 pages.

Un ouvrage sur l'économie québécoise contemporaine.
Disponible en bibliothèque.

(S)   Panitch, L., (ed) **The Canadian State: Political Economy and Political Power,** University of Toronto Press, Toronto, 1977, 470 pages.

A collection of essays examining the role of the state in the political economy of Canada. Available on order from your local bookstore or library.

Centralized Economy

Economic power has also been concentrated and centralized in the two major metropolitan centers, namely Toronto and Montreal. Deliberate choices have been made to locate the country's largest corporations, financial institutions, and most of the manufacturing industries in Toronto, Montreal, and to a much lesser extent, Winnipeg, Calgary, Edmonton and Vancouver. Historically, the economic development of the country has been largely determined by the industrial interests of Montreal and Toronto. In recent years, the center of economic power has shifted from Montreal to Toronto. It is now estimated, for example, that 45 percent of all American-owned industry in Canada, is located in the greater metropolitan Toronto area. This centralization of economic power continues to be largely responsible for the very uneven patterns of development and the regional disparities that exist across the country today.

The Church and the Economic Order

The transformation of the economic order in our society continues to be a major issue for discussion and debate in the life of the Church. The following are some recent examples.

—The Canadian bishops have in recent years, issued pastoral statements reflecting an ethical critique of modern capitalism and calling for the transformation of our economic order. See, **From Words to Action,** 1976 Labour Day message; **A Society to be Transformed,** 1977 social message. Available at cost from the Canadian Conference of Catholic Bishops, Publication Service, 90 Parent Avenue, Ottawa, Ontario, K1N 7B1.

—Ecumenically, the Churches have also worked together in developing a critical perspective on the present economic order. See, for example, **Justice Demands Action** (1976 Brief of Church leaders to federal government) and the **Inter-church Brief on Economic Outlook** (1978 Brief to federal government).

—Regionally, the Church has also begun to develop a critical awareness of the economic order in Canada. The Atlantic bishops, for example, have recently released a statement, **To Establish a Kingdom of Justice,** which critically assesses the economic and political forces that have caused the underdevelopment of the Atlantic region.

—The Social Affairs Department of the Canadian Conference of Catholic Bishops continues to develop a critical analysis of our economic order, from the standpoint of Gospel values, and examine alternative economic models. At the same time, several Church-sponsored action-research projects at national and regional levels are continuing to develop a more in-depth analysis concerning the structural problems of our economic order. And, in a variety of ways, increasing numbers of Christians are becoming involved in discussion and debate about the transformation of our economic order.

2. Political Order

Enlightened politics also demands that men rise above the level of passion, and take account of the truth that political regimes and legal structures are means, not ends, and therefore susceptible, as history shows, of constant reform.
(Canadian Bishops, **A Letter on the 100th Anniversary of Confederation,** *1967)*

The political order of Canada, as well as the economic order, is plagued by some basic structural problems. In a myriad of ways, people are faced with problems of exercising political self-determination. For many, the political structures of Canada tend to inhibit rather than enhance the self-determination of peoples with respect to their own economic, cultural, and social affairs. Internally, the movement for independence in Quebec has dramatized the inadequacies of Canada's political structures and the limitations of political self-determination in the present system. Externally, Canada and its regions have become trapped in a situation of political as well as economic dependency on the United States. In the midst of these realities, there are other structural problems such as the distribution of federal and provincial powers, the political development of the North, the close ties between economic and political power, the powerlessness of popular and marginalized groups.

Canada's Political Experiment

For some people, Canada represents a unique political experiment. Through Confederation, the colonies of British North America were forged into a new nation state, based on the union of two societies, with a strong central government. Yet, the historical experience since Confederation has shown that the Canadian political experiment has benefited some regions and peoples at the expense of others. The union between a largely anglophone society and a largely francophone society has been unequal, with the former dominating the latter. Excluded from this political union were the original peoples themselves, namely the Indian and the Inuit. Through this political experiment, the provinces of central Canada also benefited economically at the expense of other regions. Not only in Quebec, but in the Maritimes and the Prairies, there are reasons to question the roots and effects of Confederation.

Bilodeau, R., et alii, **Histoire des deux Canada,** Hurtubise, HMH, 1971, 676 pages.

Un ouvrage-synthèse sur l'histoire du Québec et du Canada. Disponible en librairie.

(S) Creighton, D., **Canada's First Century: 1867-1967,** MacMillan Company, Toronto, 1970, 372 pages.

An historical overview of Canada's political experiment. Available on order from your local bookstore or library.

(S) Hodgkings and Page (editors), **Canadian History Since Confederation: Essays and Interpretations,** Georgetown, Ontario, 1972.

A collection of interpretative essays on Canada's political experiment since Confederation. Available on order from your local bookstore or library.

(S) Ryerson, S.B., **Unequal Union: Confederation and the Roots of Conflict in Canada,** 1815-1873, Progress Books. 1978, 477 pages.

This study analyzes the roots of Québec's discontent with Confederation. Available on order from your local bookstore.

Political Self-Determination of Quebec Society

The current struggle for political self-determination in Quebec has deep historical roots. In effect, they go back before Confederation to the Conquest of 1763, which marked the end of French colonization and the beginning of British colonialism in Canada. Thereafter, the people of Quebec lost a significant measure of control over the economic, political and cultural affairs of their society. While in the past two centuries, Quebec has been gradually transformed from an agricultural-based society to a modern industrial society, some of the basic problems of colonialism remain. The Quebec economy, for example, is still largely dominated by foreign-owned corporations. In the "Quiet Revolution" of the early 1960's, the slogan "Maîtres chez-nous" — masters in our own home — gave expression to a new spirit and a new era. With a new consciousness of their history and their culture, les Québécois are striving to build a new society in which the people of Quebec will have control over their own political, economic and cultural affairs.

(S) Bergeron, G., **Le Canada français après deux siècles de patience,** Seuil, Paris, 1967, 275 pages.

Un ouvrage classique sur l'évolution du Québec. Disponible en bibliothèque.

(S) Brunelle, D., **La désillusion tranquille,** Hurtubise, HMH, collection "Cahiers du Québec", Montréal, 1978, 225 pages.

Une étude qui s'attache aux aspects moins connus de la révolution tranquille. Disponible en librairie.

(S) Fréchette, P., et alii, **L'économie du Québec,** les Editions HRW, Montréal, 1975, 436 pages.

Un ouvrage sur l'économie québécoise contemporaine, ses forces et ses faiblesses. Disponible en librairie.

(S) M.D.C.P.D., **Le Québec contemporain,** document de référence au Congrès du Mouvement des caisses populaires Desjardins, congrès régional, juillet 1977, 277 pages.

Un document-synthèse sur la société québécoise. On y retrouve des chapitres sur la démographie, l'économie et le domaine socio-culturel. Disponible en bibliothèque.

(S) Milner S. and H., **The Decolonization of Québec,** MacMillan and Stewart, Toronto, 1973.

An analysis of the historical roots of the current movements for social change in Québec. Available on order from your local bookstore or library.

(S)(A) Québec: **A Province "Pas comme les autres",** Issue No. 11, United Church of Canada Publication, Toronto, 1976, 6 pages.

A popular overview of the current movements in Quebec society. Available on order from the United Church of Canada, 85 St Clair Avenue East, Toronto, Ontario.

(S) Roy, J.L., **La marche des Québécois, le temps des ruptures,** Ottawa, Leméac, 1976, 383 pages.

L'évolution socio-économique du Québec sous les gouvernements Duplessis: une analyse des bases de la révolution tranquille. Disponible en librairie.

Political Self-Determination of Canadian Society

The independence of Canada, as a nation state, poses another structural problem. Indeed, some probing questions have been raised about the capacities of Canadian society itself to effectively exercise political self-determination over its own economic, cultural and social affairs. Historically, Canada too has had its own colonial experience. Following Confederation, the building of an industrial society in this country was initially dominated by the interests of the British Empire. In this century, the social, economic, and cultural affairs of Canada have been largely shaped and determined by the United States. The dominant influence of American culture on the values and life-styles of Canadian society and the increasing control of American-based corporations over the economy, are indicative of Canada's vulnerable position as an independent state. Nevertheless, in the past decade, there have been signs that some Canadians are taking a more critical look at the problems of political self-determination.

(S)   Beauregard, D., **A qui appartient le Canada?,** Stanké Ltée, Montréal, 1978, 224 pages.

Une analyse de l'influence américaine sur la vie socio-économique au Canada. Disponible en librairie ou bibliothèque.

(S)   Clement, W., **Continental Corporate Power: Economic Linkages Between Canada and the United States,** McClelland and Stewart, Toronto, 1977, 408 pages.

A study of the structures of Canada's economic and political dependency on the United States. Available on order from your local bookstore or library.

(S)   Grant, G., **Lament for a Nation,** McClelland and Stewart, Toronto, 1965.

An analysis of the erosion of Canada's political independence during the sixties. Available on order from your local library.

(S)   Hardin, H., **A Nation Unaware: The Canadian Economic Culture,** Vancouver, 1974.

An overview of the problems of cultural survival facing Canada. Available on order from your local bookstore or library.

(S)   Rotstein A., (ed.) **Independence: The Canadian Challenge,** McClelland and Stewart, Toronto, 1972, 279 pages.

A collection of articles explaining different aspects of Canada's economic and political dependency on the United States. Available on order from your local library.

Federal and Provincial Powers

The distribution of federal and provincial powers reveals another set of problems in Canada's political order. Through the constitution, the federal government assumed strong centralized powers to oversee the complete development of Canada. The past two decades, however, have witnessed a noticeable shift in federal and provincial powers. The provinces have taken over several fields of government affairs previously under federal jurisdiction, enlarged provincial bureaucracy and expenditures, and increased their own taxing powers. A major factor in this shift has been the direct involvement of provincial governments in the development and export of natural resources (minerals, timber, petroleum, hydro power, etc.). As a result, there has been a strengthening of regional and cultural loyalties along with closer economic and political ties with corresponding regions in the United States. Indeed, co-operation or co-ordination between the provinces and the federal government has deteriorated.

(S)   **Le Canada et le Québec: bilan et prospective,** numéro spécial de la revue **Etudes internationales,** vol. VIII, no 3, juin 1977, Centre québécois de relations internationales, Québec.

Un dossier sur l'aspect constitutionnel du débat: les forces en présence; la politique étrangère en devenir. Disponible en bibliothèque ou en s'adressant au Centre québécois de relations internationales, Faculté des sciences sociales, Université Laval, Québec, G1K 7P4.

(S) Meekison, J.P., **Canadian Federalism: Myth or Reality,** Second Edition, Methuen, Toronto, 1971.

A collection of essays on the myth and realities of Canadian federalism. Available on order at your local bookstore or library.

(S) Morin, C., **Le pouvoir québécois en négociations,** les Editions Boréal Express, Québec, 1972.

L'évolution des relations Québec-Ottawa au cours des anNées 1960. Disponible en librairie.

(S) Pépin and Robarts, **A Future Together,** Government of Canada. 1979.

Report of the Task Force on Canadian Unity, including some current observations and recommendations on Canadian federalism. Available on order at your local bookstore or library.

(S) Simeon, R., (ed.) **Must Canada Fail?,** McGill-Queen's University Press, Montréal-London, 1977.

A collection of articles dealing with the current constitutional debate. Available on order at your local bookstore.

(S) Veilleux, G., **Les relations inter-gouvernementales au Canada,** les Presses de l'Université du Québec, Montréal, 1971.

Une analyse des relations fédérales-provinciales et des mécanismes de ces relations. Disponible en librairie.

Political Development of the North

The political order of Canada is further being challenged by the Native peoples of the North who have never surrendered their aboriginal rights to the lands in northern Canada. The Yukon and the Northwest Territories, which have been the traditional homeland of Indian and Inuit peoples, continue to be governed by the federal government in Ottawa. For the Native peoples, the territorial councils are a form of colonial government in the North. Today, the Native peoples are asserting their rights to political self-determination through the land-claims negotiations with the federal government. In the Northwest Territories, for example, the Dene have declared themselves to be an aboriginal nation within Canada and have called for the establishment of their own political, economic, social and cultural institutions to serve the needs of their people. Similar positions are being advanced by the Inuit in the Eastern Arctic and the Indians of the Yukon.

(S) Badcock, W., **Who owns Canada? Aboriginal Title and the Canadian Courts,** Canadian Association in Support of Native Peoples, Ottawa, 1976, 39 pages.

An analysis of the Native peoples' claim to aboriginal title in the context of Canada's constitution and courts. Available on order from the Canadian Association in Support of Native Peoples, 251 Laurier Avenue W., Ottawa, Ontario, K1P 5J6.

(S) Berger, T., **Northern Frontier, Northern Homeland,** (Vol. 1), Mackenzie Valley Pipeline Inquiry Report, Minister of Supply and Services, Canada, Ottawa, 1977, 213 pages.

A comprehensive study that deals with the Native peoples' aspirations for political self-determination in the North. Available on order from your local bookstore or library.

(S) Cummings, R., & Mickenburg, **Native Rights in Canada,** General Publishing Co., Toronto, 1972.

A study on the aboriginal rights of Native peoples in Canada. Available on order from your local library.

(S)   Watkins, M., (ed.), **Dene Nation: A Colony Within,** University of Toronto Press, Toronto, 1977, 189 pages.

A collection of articles and statements pertaining to the political aspirations of the Dene peoples in the Northwest Territories. Available on order from your local bookstore or library.

Economic and Political Power

The close alliance between economic and political power in Canada poses another set of structural problems. Historically, there has been a close working relationship between business and political leaders. Indeed, they have often been the same people. Since the second world war, studies show that there has been an increasing penetration of representatives from the business sector in key positions of both the civil service bureaucracies and the cabinets of federal and provincial governments. As a result, the political leadership and bureaucracy of the country is drawn from a narrow socio-economic base, and is thereby more and more removed from popular control. Moreover, faced with the expanding powers of transnational corporations, there are signs that federal and provincial governments are becoming relatively powerless in their role of protecting the needs of people.

(S)   Clement, W., **The Canadian Corporate Elite,** Carleton Library No. 89, McClelland and Stewart, 1975, 479 pages.

Includes an analysis of the links between economic and political power in Canada. Available on order from your local bookstore or library.

(S)   Fournier, P., **The Québec Establishment,** Black Rose Books, Montréal, 1976.

A study that shows the structural connections between economic and political power in Quebec. Available on order from your local bookstore or library.

(S)   Newman. P., **The Canadian Establishment** (Vol. 1), McClelland and Stewart Co., Toronto, 1975, 390 pages.

A profile of leading businessmen who constitute Canada's "non-elected government". Available on order from your local bookstore or library.

(S)   Porter, J., **The Vertical Mosaic,** University of Toronto Press, 1965.

A somewhat dated but major study of the class structures of Canada. Available on order from your local bookstore or library.

Powerless Groups

Underlying many of these concerns about our political order is the problem of powerlessness experienced by popular and marginalized groups. For the most part, our political structures are not based on an equitable representation of all classes and cultures in society. As a result, working people, the poorest sectors of the population plus many cultural and racial groups, are not adequately represented in the decisions on public policy affecting their lives. In some cases, the powerlessness experienced by these marginalized groups has led to increasing alienation, apathy, dependency and even violence. In some other cases, groups of workers, citizens, or cultural minorities have been able to organize themselves to exercise political self-determination in changing the social and economic conditions in which they live and work.

The Current Debate on Political Options in the Church

The political future of Quebec and Canada continues to be a major issue for discussion and debate in the life of the Church. The following are some examples:

—The Canadian bishops have published two statements in a document entitled, **Various Political Options in Canada** ("A Letter on the 100th Anniversary of Confederation", 1967, and "Pastoral Implications of Political Choices", 1972). Available on order, at cost from the Publication Service, Canadian Conference of Catholic Bishops, 90 Parent Avenue, Ottawa, K1N 7B1.

—The bishops' statements have been analyzed and debated in various articles. See, for example: Desrochers, I., "Les évêques canadiens et la vie politique au Québec, dans **Relations,** juin 1972; L'église catholique et l'unité canadienne", dans **Relations,** avril 1978; "L'oécuménisme et l'unité canadienne", dans **Relations,** mai 1978.

—In some other regions of the country, bishops have recently issued statements. For example, the Alberta bishops published a statement (see **La Voix,** Archdiocese of Grouard-McLennan, February, 1978) and the bishops of British Columbia submitted a statement to the Pépin-Robarts Commission (see **B.C. Catholic,** February 1978).

—The Canadian Conference of Catholic Bishops and l'Assemblée des évêques du Québec continue to monitor, in various ways, the current debate about the political future of Canada and Québec. And, in Québec, several dioceses have initiated projects to assist people in reflecting on various political options in the light of Gospel values (contact, for example, l'Office de pastorale sociale, diocèse de Québec, 1073 St-Cyrille ouest, Québec, G1S 4B5).

3. Continuing Poverty

"...the riches of Canada are unequally shared. This inequality which keeps so many people poor, is a social sin".
*(Canadian Bishops, **Sharing National Income,** 1972)*

For many people, Canada appears to be a relatively affluent society with equal opportunity for all its citizens. Yet, the fact that one out of four families in Canada continues to live in poverty directly contradicts this perception of reality. Indeed, the continuing presence of such poverty in the midst of affluence dramatizes the basic inequalities that continue to oppress people in our society.

People in Poverty

Out of the five million people living in poverty conditions in Canada today, close to two and a half million are working people and their families. The working poor include seasonal workers like fishermen, woodcutters, and farm labourers, or people who work in small assembly shops, garment factories or cafeterias. In the face of rising prices, they are trying desperately to support their families on low annual wages. The remaining two and a half million people living in poverty are mainly composed of the elderly, single parents, the physically and mentally handicapped. These are the welfare poor who, for the most part, are unable to work. Supported by welfare schemes, they often suffer from the stigma of living off government handouts and the problems of dependency. Along with the working poor, they are also faced with the added burden of current government cut-backs in health care and related social and educational services. And while government welfare schemes help to alleviate the physical suffering, they also have the negative effect of maintaining people in positions of dependency and powerlessness.

(S) Girouard, A., **L'appauvrissement des petits salariés,** (résumé), Montréal, Centre des services sociaux du Montréal métropolitain, 1977, 112 pages.

Une étude en profondeur des conditions socio-économiques des petits salariés vivant dans un grand centre urbain. Disponible en écrivant au Centre des services sociaux du Montréal métropolitain, 800 boul. de Maisonneuve est, Montréal, Québec.

(A) **Les assistés sociaux et le monde ouvrier,** Dossiers "vie ouvrière", no 108, octobre 1976.

Une série d'articles sur les assistés sociaux et le monde ouvrier. Disponible en écrivant à Dossier "vie ouvrière", 1201 rue Visitation, Montréal, H2L 3B5.

(A) **Poor Kids,** Report of the National Council of Welfare, Ottawa, 1975, 67 pages.

A report on children in poverty in Canada. Available by writing to the National Council of Welfare, Brooke Claxton Building, Ottawa, K1A 0K9.

(S)(A)   Ross, D., **Canadian Fact Book on Poverty,** Canadian Council for Social Development, Ottawa, 1975, 32 pages.

          A booklet outlining the basic facts on poverty in Canada. Available from the Canadian Council for Social Development, 55 Parkdale Avenue, Ottawa, K1Y 4G1.

(S)(A)   **The Working Poor,** National Council of Welfare, Ottawa, 1977, 30 pages.

          A statistical profile of the working poor. Available from the National Council of Welfare, Brooke Claxton Building, Ottawa, K1A 0K9.

Class Division

The realities of poverty in the midst of affluence illustrate the serious divisions that exist between social classes. Gross disparities persist in the distribution of wealth and power in our society. Today, the top 20% of income earners receive 43% of the total personal income in this country while the bottom 20% receive less than 4% (Statistics Canada, 1977). At the same time, the ownership of the means for producing wealth (i.e. investment assets like stocks, bonds, real estate, etc.) is concentrated in the hands of less than 10% of the population. This pattern of disparity has remained virtually the same for the past quarter of a century. Yet, these class divisions result in social tensions between rich and poor, powerful and powerless in our society.

(S)   Clement, Wallace, **Canadian Corporate Elite,** Carleton Library, No. 89, McClelland and Stewart Ltd., Toronto, 1975, 479 pages.

          An up-to-date major sociological study on wealth and power in Canada. Available in paperback from your local bookstore.

(S)(A)   Johnson, Leo, **Poverty in Wealth,** New Hogtown Press, Toronto, 1974.

          A pamphlet analyzing class divisions in terms of income distribution in Canada. Available on order from the Development Education Centre, 121 Avenue Road, Toronto.

(S)   Myers, G., **A History of Canadian Wealth,** James Lorimer and Company, Toronto, 1975.

          An historical analysis concerning the accumulation of wealth in Canada. Available on order from your local bookstore or library.

(S)   Sennet and Cobb, **The Hidden Injuries of Class,** Knopf, New York, 1972.

          Discusses the human and social injuries that result from class structures in modern society. Available on order from your local bookstore or library.

Maintaining Poverty

For the most part, the poor are poor, not because they choose to be, but because they have not other choice. Indeed, the poor are the casualties of the way we have chosen to manage our economy. As the 1971 Senate Poverty Report states, "the economic system in which most people prosper is the same system which creates poverty." The trickle-down theory of economic growth, which contends that the wealth produced by our economy is eventually redistributed for the benefit of all people, is a fallacy. Indeed, there are mechanisms in our economic system which maintain and increase poverty. In 1968, for example, the Carter Commission on Taxation reported that the poor are overtaxed relative to their income. They pay a higher proportion of their income on taxes of all kinds, than do upper income groups. And, more recent studies show that, in the past fifteen years, the percentage of income taxes paid by corporations has been steadily falling while the percentage of personal income taxes (of which workers contribute a large share) have been steadily rising.

(S)   Adams, I., and others, **The Real Poverty Report,** M.G. Hurtig Ltd. Publishers, Edmonton, 1971, 255 pages.

The minority report issued by the researchers who worked on the Senate Poverty Report. Available on order from your local bookstore.

(S)(A)   **Bearing the Burden/Sharing the Benefits,** National Council of Welfare, Ottawa, 1978, 30 pages.

A report on taxation and the distribution of income. Available by writing to the National Council of Welfare, Brooke Claxton Building, Ottawa, K1A 0K9.

(S)   **Senate Poverty Report,** Queen's Printer, Ottawa, 1971.

The controversial study of the Senate documenting some of the basic realities of poverty in Canada. Available on order from your local bookstore or library.

(A)   **The Economics of Injustice,** Issue No. 10, United Church of Canada Publication, Toronto, 1975, 4 pages.

A popular overview of the realities and structures of poverty in Canada. Available from the United Church of Canada, 85 St Clair Avenue East, Toronto.

(S)(A)   **The Hidden Welfare System,** National Council of Welfare, Ottawa, 1976, 38 pages.

A report on the personal income tax system in Canada. Available by writing to the National Council of Welfare, Brooke Claxton Building, Ottawa, K1A 0K9.

Some Christian Education-Action Programmes

In recent years, there has been a shift on the part of some Christian groups in addressing the problems of poverty. While continuing to sponsor social service programmes, the Church has become more actively involved in increasing the capacities of poor people's groups engaged in struggles to change the conditions and causes of poverty. In co-operation with the National Anti-Poverty Organization for example, PLURA was organized as an ecumenical programme of the churches to provide funds for local and regional people's groups striving to bring about social changes. The Churches have also supported various anti-poverty organizations by continually urging the federal government to make major changes in social security programmes and tax legislation. At the same time, Christian groups in several dioceses across the country have been working in solidarity with local poor people's organizations. In a variety of ways, these Christian groups are engaged in supporting tenants'unions, welfare recipients, and anti-poverty organizations in their particular struggles and assisting them in analyzing and reflecting on the causes of poverty.

*For more information, contact: PLURA, c/o 90 Parent Avenue, Ottawa, K1N 7B1 (Tel. 613-236-9461, ext. 236); National Anti-Poverty Organization, 196 Bronson Avenue, Ottawa, Ontario (Tel. 613-238-6311).

Some Questions For Animators

1. What are some of the specific examples of conditions of poverty in your community? or region? Have you or your group had any practical experience in educating and acting on these problems?

2. What kinds of research or studies have been done on the realities of poverty in your community or region? What have been the conclusions? What are the basic causes of poverty in your community or region?

3. What critical insights can be found in the Scriptures or the social teachings of the Church? What specific ethical or theological judgments can be made about the injustices of poverty and its causes?

4. What can be done to develop a critical awareness among Christians in your community on the problems and causes of poverty? What kinds of animation methods and tools are necessary and useful?

5. Are there any organized poor people's groups in your community or region trying to bring about some changes? Tenants' unions? Anti-poverty organizations? What kind of co-operation or working relationships could be developed with these groups?

6. What relevant connections can be made between the problems and causes of poverty in Canada and the realities of poverty in the Third World? What are some of the similarities and differences?

7. What kinds of actions can be taken by Christian groups to support the struggles of poor people's groups to change their oppressive conditions?

4. Industrial Exploitation

"...Across the land there has been a heightening of industrial strife... The economic and political system have come under attack not only because so many workers are denied incomes commensurate with corporate earnings and government revenues, but also because men and women are denied an effective share in decision-making".
(Canadian Bishops, **Simplicity and Sharing,** *1972)*

In the building of an industrial society in Canada, workers have been largely responsible for producing the wealth in this country. Yet, workers in Canada have long been denied a fair share of the wealth produced and have been subjected to other forms of exploitation. While some workers, through unions, have struggled and achieved significant gains, many more workers are still subjected to a variety of injustices.

Increasing Layoffs

Approximately a million people out of a labour force of 10.3 million, are out of work, the largest number of unemployed in our history. Faced with increasing layoffs, thousands of workers are being deprived of a basic human right, namely, the right to work. The rising rate of unemployment hits certain people (e.g. women and young people) more than others and is concentrated in certain regions (e.g. the Atlantic provinces) of the country. Indeed, people working in low-paying jobs without job security, are the most vulnerable to layoffs in these times of economic recession.

While the more immediate causes of unemployment are related to the current economic recession, the roots of the problem appear to be in the industrial strategies of our economy. To increase profits and maximize efficiency, for example, many industries have re-oriented the capital produced into new production technologies that require less human labour. In the management of Canada's economy, a priority has been put on investment in resource industries, which are capital-intensive, relying more on machinery than on people and tools. Meanwhile, Canada's manufacturing sector, which is labour intensive, and produces (along with the service sectors) most of the jobs in our economy, has remained relatively weak and underdeveloped. Indeed, the foreign ownership of Canada's manufacturing and resource industries has left our economy in a particularly vulnerable position. Several American-owned industries, for example, have been shifting their production back to plants in the United States, thereby exporting thousands of jobs. At the same time, some Canadian mining companies have been shifting production to several Third World countries to take advantage of cheap labour conditions and other incentives, thereby laying off thousands of Canadian workers.

(S)(A) Carty, R., **Layoffs in Canada's Mining Industry,** Latin American Working Group, Toronto, 1978, 25 pages.

A recent analysis of layoffs in Canada's mining industries and shifting patterns of production to certain Third World countries. Available on order from the Latin American Working Group, Box 2207, Station P, Toronto, Ontario, M5R 2T2.

(S)(A) **Dignity Denied: Unemployment in Canada,** Canadian News Synthesis Project, Toronto, 1976, 6 pages.

A report on the current unemployment crisis and its effect on workers. Available from Development Education Centre, 121 Avenue Road, Toronto, Ontario, M5R 2G3.

(S)(A) McGrath, D. et al., **Now That We've Burned Our Boats....** The Report of Peoples' Commission on Unemployment, Newfoundland and Labrador, Mutual Press, Ottawa, June, 1978, 117 pages.

A popular, illustrated analysis of the problems and the causes of unemployment in Newfoundland and Labrador, Federation of Labour, 77 Bond Street, Room 206, St. John's, Newfoundland.

(A) **Quand ferment les usines,** Dossiers "vie ouvrière", no 117, Montréal, 1977.

Une série d'articles sur les fermetures d'usines au Québec. Disponible à Dossiers "vie ouvrière", 1201 rue Visitation, Montréal, H2L 3B5.

(A) **Unemployment,** Issue No. 18, United Church of Canada Publication, Toronto, April 1978, 6 pages.

A popular overview of the causes of unemployment in Canada today. Available by writing to the United Church of Canada, 85 St Clair Avenue East, Toronto.

Exploitation of Workers

In many industries today, workers are still subjected to various forms of exploitation. **Cheap labour:** Poor immigrants and women form a pool of cheap labour taking low-paying jobs in small shops, factories, cafeterias, and other industries where others refuse to work because of the conditions. Through contract-labour schemes, employers bring in immigrant workers from poorer countries to fill low-paying jobs in agriculture, construction and mining industries on a short-term basis. While minimum wage laws exist in all the provinces, the legislation is seldom enforced. **Poor Working Conditions:** Workers are still subject to poor working conditions in several industries today. Asbestos workers and coal workers, for example, are subjected to the constant threat of serious lung disease while workers in "sweat" factories and on assembly lines often find their work demeaning and dehumanizing. While health and safety standards now exist, they are often inadequate or poorly enforced. **Monopoly Control:** Many small producers, in addition to industrial workers, are also experiencing forms of exploitation. Large corporations, which have secured control over markets and prices, have been forcing many small farmers, fishermen, and businessmen out of operation, thereby making them give up their livelihood.

(S) Girouard, A., **L'appauvrissement des petits salariés,** (résumé), Montréal, Centre des services sociaux du Montréal métropolitain, 1977, 112 pages.

Une étude en profondeur des conditions socio-économiques des petits salariés vivant dans un grand centre urbain. Disponible en écrivant au Centre des services sociaux du Montréal métropolitain, 800 boul. de Maisonneuve est, Montréal, Québec.

(A) **Inshore/Offshore**

A slide-tape presentation showing the demise of the fishing industry in the Atlantic region. Available on order from the Development Education Centre, 121 Avenue Road, Toronto, Ontario, M5R 2G3.

(A) **Le sang des ouvriers: les accidents de travail,** Dossiers "vie ouvrière", no 75, Montréal, mai 1975, 62 pages.

Une série d'articles sur les accidents de travail. Disponible en écrivant à Dossiers "vie ouvrière", 1201 rue Visitation, Montréal, Québec, H2L 3B5.

(A) **Les conditions de travail et la vie familiale,** Dossiers "vie ouvrière", no 88, Montréal, Québec.

Une série d'articles sur les conditions de travail et la vie familiale. Disponible à Dossiers "vie ouvrière", 1201 rue Visitation, Montréal, Québec, H2L 3B5.

(A) **Les ouvrières du vêtement,** Dossiers "vie ouvrière", no 116, juin 1977, Montréal, 61 pages.

Une série d'articles sur les conditions de travail des ouvrières du vêtement. Disponible en écrivant à Dossiers "vie ouvrière", 1201 rue Visitation, Montréal, Québec, H2L 3B5.

(A) **Work We Will Not Do...** Issue No. 7, United Church of Canada Publication, Toronto, 1975, 4 pages.

A popular analysis of the exploitation of migrant and immigrant workers in Canada. Available by writing to the United Church of Canada, 85 St Clair Avenue East, Toronto, Ontario.

Control of Workers

In recent years, workers have found themselves facing legislated controls by federal and provincial governments, which, in effect, have served to undercut the long struggle of workers for better wages and working conditions. While recent wage and price controls affected all people in Canada, wage controls had their heaviest impact on workers. The wages of workers were more strictly regulated than the prices of most commodities. As a result, corporate profits continued to rise while the wages of workers were stabilized. At the same time, various government cutbacks in social services (for example, health, education, housing, etc.) have also had a major impact on workers and the poorer sectors of the population.

Taken together, these measures serve to wipe out many of the gains that workers have achieved in the past and make it increasingly difficult to cope with inflation and cost of living increases. Moreover, less than 40% of Canada's paid workers (outside of agriculture) are members of organized unions, leaving a large number of workers unorganized and unable to struggle for better wages and working conditions. In some industries, employers still use a variety of means to prevent workers from organizing unions and in some cases the unions themselves have not given sufficient attention to the plight of unorganized workers.

(A)   **Concentration ou confrontation,** Dossiers "vie ouvrière", no 118, Montréal, 1977.

Une analyse du sommet économique entre le gouvernement et les travailleurs du Québec. Disponible à Dossiers "vie ouvrière", 1021 rue Visitation, Montréal, Québec, H2L 3B5.

(A)   **Cutbacks: Wiping Out Our Gains,** GATT-Fly Project, Toronto, 1977, 8 pages.

A short pamphlet, analyzing cutbacks in social services in Ontario, but applicable to most provinces. Available by writing to GATT-Fly Project, 11 Madison Avenue, Toronto, Ontario, M5R 2S2.

(S)   **Histoire des organisations syndicales,** Dossiers "vie ouvrière", no 111, janvier 1977, Montréal, 64 pages.

Un recueil d'articles sur les syndicats, les ouvriers et les grèves historiques au Québec. Disponible en écrivant à Dossiers "vie ouvrière", 1201 rue Visitation, Montréal, Québec, H2L 3B5.

(S)   Lipton, D., **The Trade Union Movement of Canada 1826-1959,** Toronto, NC Press, 3rd Edition, 1975, 384 pages.

A history of the labour movement's progress throughout 130 years of Canadian history. Available on order from your local bookstore.

(A)   Popular Economics Group, **Inflation and Democracy in Canada: Thirty Years of Stop and Go,** DGP Publishers, Kitchener, 1976, 22 pages.

A pamphlet examining inflation and unemployment in Canada and assessing the impact of wage and price controls. Available from Development Education Centre, 121 Avenue Road, Toronto, M5R 2G3.

(S)(A)   **Problèmes de législation ouvrière,** Dossiers "vie ouvrière", nos 106 et 107, Montréal, 1976.

Deux numéros consacrés aux problèmes de législation ouvrière. Disponibles à Dossiers "vie ouvrière", 1201 rue Visitation, Montréal, Québec, H2L 3B5.

(A)   **Témiscaming, Québec,** 16 m/m film, National Film Board, 1975, 2 parts, (Part I: 31 min., Part II: 33 min.).

Portrays the effort of workers and their community to gain more control over an industry. Available on order from the National Film Board Library closest to your area.

Some Christian Education-Action Projects

Through groups like the Christian Workers' Movement, the Church has had a history of direct involvement with the struggles of workers in various parts of the country. Today, the Christian Workers' Movement is most active in Québec where different Christian worker groups are actively involved with the labour movement. The bishops of Quebec in recent years, have made the struggle of workers for justice in Quebec a major pastoral priority. Le Mouvement des travailleurs chrétiens, which is sponsored by the Quebec bishops, is an example of a Christian group involved in worker struggles. MTC groups are active in various communities throughout Quebec supporting workers on several issues and each month, the MTC publishes "Présence", documenting specific cases of worker exploitation along with theological reflection on the issues. Outside of Quebec, the Extension Department of St Francis Xavier University in Nova Scotia has been directly involved in supporting the struggles of wood-cutters, fishermen and other workers in the Maritimes. In the Maritimes, Christian groups are working with coalitions for full employment in Sydney, Glace Bay, and Halifax, providing various forms of support and helping people to reflect on the causes of unemployment. And, in Newfoundland, local Christian leaders recently participated with the Newfoundland Federation of Labour in organizing a major public inquiry into the problems and causes of unemployment and published a full report entitled, "Now That We've Burned Our Boats". (See reference above).

*For more information, contact: Mouvement des travailleurs chrétiens, 7559 boul. St-Joseph, Montréal, Québec (Tel. 514-274-2667); see also, le Centre de pastorale en milieu ouvrier, 1212 rue Panet, Montréal, Québec (Tel. 514-524-3561). For information on the Quebec bishops' statements, contact: le Bureau des affaires sociales, Assemblée des évêques du Québec, 1225 est, boul. Saint-Joseph, Montréal, Québec, H2J 1L7 (Tel. 514-272-1179).

Some Questions For Animators

1. What are some of the specific labour struggles going on in your community or region? Lock-outs? Poor working conditions? Job insecurity? Cheap labour? Non-unionized workers? Lay-offs? Plant shut-downs? Small producers being forced out of business? Others? Has your group had any practical experience in educating or acting on these issues?

2. What kinds of research or studies have been done on industrial development strategies in your community or region? What impact has new industrial development had on creating jobs? The wages of workers? The economic base of the region?

3. What critical insights can be appropriated from the Scriptures and the social teachings concerning the struggles of workers for justice? What ethical or theological judgments can be made about the exploitation of workers?

4. What can be done to develop the critical awareness of Christians in your community concerning struggles for justice on the part of local workers? What kinds of animation methods and tools would be necessary or useful?

5. What kind of co-operation or working relationships could be developed with local labour unions, coalitions for full employment, other organizations dealing with problems of industrial exploitation?

6. What relevant connections can be made between examples of industrial exploitation in your region and similar problems in other regions of the country? In the Third World?

7. What kinds of actions could be taken by Christian groups in your community to support particular local struggles of workers, small producers, or the unemployed for justice?

5. Production and Needs

*"...the present food market is primarily designed to make profits,
not to feed people."*
(Canadian Bishops, **Sharing Daily Bread,** *1974)*

*"...while the sale of these resources will reap large profits for the energy industry
now, it may also cause the rapid depletion of non-renewable supplies of oil and gas
required for the future."*
(Canadian Bishops, **Northern Development: At What Cost?** *1975)*

*"...Our task, therefore, is to define clearly the links we wish between profit,
consumption and the quality of life for us all: housing for people, or housing for
profits?"*
(Canadian Bishops, **Decent Housing for All,** *1976)*

Canada is a country blessed with an abundance of natural resources that
can be developed to serve the basic human needs of all people in this country
for food, housing, employment and energy. It is becoming more and more
evident, however, that the production of food, housing, and energy in our
society is not adequately serving the needs of people, particularly the poorest
sectors of the population. In recent years, the production of food, housing, and
energy has increasingly become dominated by a relatively small number of
large corporations which exercise control in the key sectors of production and
marketing. The primary goal of these corporations is expanding profits and
growth rather than serving basic human needs. Meanwhile, these vital sectors
of production are removed from effective public intervention and control for the
common good.

Food Production

People today point to several factors indicating that our food production
system is not serving the needs of people in this country:

—valuable food-producing land in almost every province is being taken over
 for the construction of airports, industrial sites, suburban developments,
 energy corridors, and recreation areas;

—small family farms are being replaced by agri-business farms;

—high food prices are having a serious impact on consumers particularly the
 poorest sectors of the population;

—the proliferation of junk foods and chemical additives continues to diminish
 the nutritional values of people's diets; and

—increasing imports of food products indicate that Canada is rapidly
 becoming dependent on other countries for the food needs of
 our population.

In the past twenty years, a small number of large corporations have grown to
dominate Canada's system of food production. For example, studies show that
these companies exercise extensive control in every sector of the food
industry: land purchase, farm machinery, farm land, transportation, processing
plants, and the marketing of food products. Indeed, giant food corporations
today exert enormous influence over farmers, producers and consumers when
it comes to the production and distribution of food in this country.

(S)(A) **Canada's Food Trade/By Bread Alone?** GATT-Fly Project, Toronto, 1978,
4 pages.

A study of recent disturbing trends in the Canadian food trade and an
examination of more self-reliant alternatives. Available from GATT-Fly Project,
11 Madison Avenue, Toronto, Ontario, M5R 2S3.

(A) **Give Us This Day Our Daily Bread,** Ten Days for World Development,
Toronto, 1978.

A collection of eleven articles for group leaders showing injustices of the food
production system in Canada and the Third World. Available on order from Ten
Days for World Development, 600 Jarvis Street, Toronto, Ontario, M4Y 2J6.

(A) **L'alimentation et l'entreprise privée,** Dossiers "vie ouvrière", no 107, Montréal, janvier 1976, 67 pages.

Une série d'articles sur l'entreprise privée et son rôle dans la production alimentaire. Disponible à Dossiers "vie ouvrière", 1201 rue Visitation, Montréal, Québec, H2L 3B5.

(A)(S) **La crise alimentaire,** (3 cahiers), Développement et Paix, Montréal, 1978.

Trois cahiers sur les problèmes posés par la présence des grands monopoles de l'agrobusiness: 1) l'origine des aliments; 2) l'agroalimentaire, empire des multinationales; 3) la terre est à tout le monde mais... Disponible à Développement et Paix, 2111 rue Centre, Montréal, Québec, H3K 1J5.

(A) **Land Use,** Issue No. 13, United Church of Canada Publication, Toronto, 1977, 4 pages.

A popular analysis of the land use problems. Available from the United Church of Canada, 85 St Clair Avenue East, Toronto, Ontario.

(S) Mitchell, D., **The Politics of Food,** James Lorimer Company, Toronto, 1975, 235 pages.

A major study on Canadian Agribusiness. Available in paperback on order from your local bookstore.

(A) **Nutrition Action.** A monthly publication of the Center for Science in the Public Interest. Provides consumers with current information and action suggestions concerning the problems of non-nutritious foods, chemical additives, and related issues about the production and consumption of food today. Available on order from Nutrition Action, 1775 S Street N.W., Washington, D.C., 20009, U.S.A.

Housing Production

People today can also point to a series of problems which illustrate that the housing system in Canada fails to serve the needs of people:

—the rising costs of housing have reached the point where the federal government now estimates that two thirds of the people who do not already own a home, cannot afford to buy one;

—real estate speculators in many cities continue to play a major role in forcing land prices upward which results in the escalating cost of housing;

—housing developers have put a priority on building high-rise apartment buildings that reap large profits but frequently result in a shortage of decent housing for families in many urban centers; and

—the materials and technology used in construction today often leave consumers with a poor quality of housing.

In effect, neither private industry nor government programmes are able to serve the housing needs of a growing number of people in Canada. As in the food industry, a small number of large development corporations exercise control over virtually every major sector of the housing industry — land surveys, land purchase, engineering design, construction, and real estate. Today, these development corporations have an enormous impact on the shaping of urban and suburban communities, the policies of municipal, provincial and federal governments, as well as the price and quality of housing itself. And while government housing programmes were originally designed to provide lower-cost housing, they have not been effective in providing a real alternative to the private housing industry.

(S) **A Review of Canadian Social Housing Policy,** Canadian Council for Social Development, 1977.

A critical look at social housing programmes of the federal and provincial governments. Available on order from the Canadian Council for Social Development, 55 Parkdale Avenue, Ottawa, K1Y 4G1.

(S)   Aubin, H., **City for Sale,** James Lorimer and Company in association with l'Etincelle, Toronto, 1978.

An analysis of the international financiers who own sections of Canada's cities. Available on order from your local bookstore.

(S)   Barker et al., **High Rise and Super Profits,** Dumont Press Graphix, Kitchener, 1973.

A useful report on the profit-making apartment construction in Canada's metropolitan areas.

(S)   Gouvernement du Québec, **Habiter au Québec,** rapport du groupe de travail sur l'habitation au Québec, (rapport Legault), Editeur officiel, Québec, 1976, 267 pages.

Une analyse en profondeur de la politique d'habitation au Québec. Disponible en bibliothèque et chez l'Editeur officiel du Québec.

(A)   **Le logement échappe aux travailleurs,** Dossiers "vie ouvrière", no 103, Montréal, mars, 1976.

Une série d'articles sur différents aspects du problème du logement. Disponible en écrivant à Dossiers "vie ouvrière", 1201 rue Visitation, Montréal, Québec, H2L 3B5.

(S)   Lorimer, J., **The Developers,** James Lorimer Company, Toronto, 1978.

An analysis of the role of large development corporations in the production of housing in Canada's major urban centers. Available on order from your local bookstore or library.

(S)   Spurr, Peter, **Land and Urban Development,** James Lorimer Company, Toronto, 1974, 437 pages.

A comprehensive study of the housing industry in Canada. Available on order from your local bookstore.

Energy Production

People are pointing to a series of problems concerning the priorities of energy production in Canada:

—the tripling of energy prices in the past five years, which has reaped billions of dollars in profits for the energy industry, but has brought further hardship to the poorest sectors of our population;

—the continuing dependence of Canada and its industrial structure on non-renewable supplies of oil and gas for over 65 percent of energy needs;

—the increasing amount of natural gas and hydro-electric power being exported to the United States;

—the high levels of per capita consumption and waste of energy in Canada, currently amongst the highest in the world;

—the reluctance to put a greater priority on developing renewable supplies of energy (sun, wind, tides, etc.) to serve future energy needs; and

—the priority being put on the development of nuclear power by federal and provincial governments, particularly the environmental and health risks associated with increasing use of nuclear reactors fueled with radio-active materials.

Today, key sectors of Canada's energy industry are controlled by foreign-owned corporations which exercise influence in almost all phases of energy production: exploration, drilling, transportation, refining and marketing. While the National Energy Board was set up to regulate the operations of these companies in the public interest, the petroleum industry still has a great deal of influence over Canada's policies, including energy prices and exports.

(S)   **An Energy Strategy for Canada,** Energy, Mines and Resources Canada, Ottawa, Minister of Supply and Services Canada, 1976, 170 pages.

The National Energy Strategy for Self-Reliance adopted by the government of Canada. Available on order from your local bookstore.

(A)   **Energy File,** Inter-church Committee on Energy, Vancouver, British Columbia.

A monthly publication on current energy issues in Canada. Available on order from Energy File, 105-2511 East Hastings Street, Vancouver, B.C., V5K 1Z2.

(S)   Gouvernement du Québec, Ministère délégué à l'énergie, **L'énergie au Québec,** Editeur officiel, Québec, 1977.

La première partie du Livre blanc sur la politique énergétique québécoise axée sur l'évolution historique de la situation québécoise. Disponible en bibliothèque.

(S)   Laxer, J., et al., **The Big Tough Expensive Job,** James Lorimer Company, Toronto.

Includes several articles analyzing the petroleum industry and federal government policies. Available on order from your local bookstore.

(S)   Laxer, J., **Canada's Energy Crisis,** James Lorimer Company, Toronto, 1975, 172 pages.

A critical analysis of Canada's energy policies. Available on order from your local bookstore.

(A)   **Nuclear Power,** Issue No. 15, United Church of Canada Publication, Toronto, April, 1977.

A useful introduction to the problems of nuclear power in Canada. Available by writing to the United Church of Canada, 85 St Clair Avenue East, Toronto, Ontario.

(A)   **The Renewal Energy Handbook,** Energy Probe, Toronto, 1976, 61 pages.

A report on the nature of energy, energy use in Canada, and possible directions for the future of Canada's energy policies. Available on order from Energy Probe, 43 Queen's Park East, Toronto.

Some Christian Education-Action Projects

The injustices revealed by the production of food, housing and energy in our society have become priorities for a variety of Christian education and action projects. While these projects are too numerous to mention, a few examples can be cited. Concerning **food** production, the Ten Days for World Development programme has helped facilitate education projects in a significant number of communities in Canada. Development and Peace, along with other Church groups, recently participated in the formation of a People's Food Commission to conduct public hearings on the injustices of Canada's food production system, involving the people who are directly engaged in growing, processing, transporting, selling, and eating food. In terms of **housing,** some dioceses and religious communities have become involved in the actual production of low-income housing and co-op housing projects while some other Christian groups have been engaged in supporting tenant unions in their struggles to change public housing projects or slum landlords. On the issues of **energy** production, Project North has assisted local and regional groups in developing education events on Canada's energy policies arising out of the debate around the construction of the Mackenzie Valley pipeline. Church sponsored groups like the Alberta Energy Coalition, the B.C. Inter-church Committee for World Development, and the Calgary Inter-faith Council have organized major educational events on the problems of energy production in Canada. And, in Saskatchewan, the bishops have taken a position on uranium development in the northern part of that province and the Inter-church Energy Coalition has waged a public campaign in opposition to specific uranium projects.

*For more information, (food) contact People's Food Commission, c/o 321 Chapel Street, Ottawa, K1N 7Z2 (Tel. 613-236-4547); Ten Days for World Development, 600 Jarvis Street, Toronto, Ontario (Tel. 416-922-0591); **(energy)** GATT-Fly Project, 11 Madison Avenue, Toronto, Ontario (Tel. 416-921-4615); Project North, 154 Glenrose Avenue, Toronto, Ontario (Tel. 416-481-3574). For information on the Church's work on uranium issues in Saskatchewan, contact the Social Action Office, Archdiocese of Regina, 3225-13th Avenue, Regina, Saskatchewan, S4T 1P5.

Some Questions For Animators

1. What are some of the major problems of food production in your community? Rising prices? Rural depopulation? Land take-overs? Quality of food? Marketing boards? Wages and working conditions for food industry workers?

2. What are some of the major problems of housing production in your community? Housing prices? Land speculation? High-rise apartments? Who are some of the major land or housing developers in your region? What impact have they had upon the building of your community?

3. Are there any large energy projects in your region? Hydro-electric developments? Pipeline projects? Uranium enrichment plants? Oil refineries? What kinds of ethical questions should be raised about these energy projects?

4. What kind of research or studies have been done on the production of food, energy, or housing in your region? What have been the conclusions? Have you or your group been involved in doing an analysis of these problems in your region?

5. What critical insights can be appropriated from the Scriptures and the social teachings of the Church? What specific ethical or theological judgments can be made about any of these issues?

6. What can be done to develop a more critical awareness on the part of Christians in your community concerning the ethical issues involved in the production of food, or housing, or energy? What kinds of animation methods and tools would be useful or necessary?

7. What kind of co-operation and working relationships could be developed with popular groups working on these questions in your community or region? e.g. farmers, fishermen, food-processing workers, or consumer groups? Local tenants' unions or citizen groups faced with land expropriation? Public interest groups concerned about problems of energy production?

8. What are the relevant connections between the problems of food production or housing or energy production in your region and elsewhere in the country? In the Third World?

9. What kinds of action could be taken by Christian groups in your community or region to support popular groups in their efforts to bring about significant changes in the production of food, or housing, or energy?

6. Regional Development

"It is evident in Canada that economic growth, and hence jobs and all social amenities, have been clustered in the Montreal-Hamilton area. What is seldom mentioned is the fact that direct policies contributed a great deal to this concentration, at the expense of other parts of the country... Canada has its own neglected 'Third World' areas..."
(**Inter-church Brief on Economic Outlook,** *1978*)

In the building of our industrial society, it is clear that certain regions have been developed at the expense of others. As industrial growth became concentrated in the metropolitan regions of central Canada, other regions of the country were designated to supply resources for the industrial centers and to provide markets for the sale of their manufactured goods. As a result, patterns of exploitation emerged in which the metropolitan industrial centers have often abused the resources and the people of the more hinterland regions.

The West

Historians remind us that the development and settlement of the western provinces was largely designed to further the economic growth of central Canada. The Prairies, for example, were opened up by grain traders in central Canada to produce wheat for export to other countries. However, both the wheat marketing system and the freight rates in transportation were designed to favour business interests of central Canada. As a result, farmers were compelled to pay high prices for the import of manufactured goods while receiving comparatively low prices for the export of their wheat. Similar patterns of exploitation affected the development of forests and mines in British Columbia. For many decades, therefore, the economies of the western provinces were developed primarily to serve the industrial interests of central Canada rather than the needs of their population. During this period, groups of farmers organized vigorous protests against these patterns of exploitation and dependence. While, in recent years, the western provinces have begun to initiate their own development strategies, the Hall Commission Report concluded that freight rates and trade structures are still decidedly in favour of the industrial centers of central Canada.

(S)(A)   Byrd, P., **Of Dust and Times and Dreams and Agonies,** Canadian News Synthesis Project, Toronto, 1975, 150 pages.

A brief social history about the building of Canada, including a descriptive account of the West. Available on order from your local bookstore.

(S)   Fowke, V., **The National Policy and the Wheat Economy,** Toronto, 1957.

A study on the development of the wheat economy in the Prairies. Available on order from your local library.

(S)   Hall, E., **Grain and Rail in Western Canada,** Hall Commission Report, Government of Canada, Queen's Printer, 1977.

A recent study on the transportation of grain and related issues. Available on order from your local bookstore.

(S) Kierans, E., **Report on Natural Resources Policy in Manitoba,** Government of Manitoba, 1973.

A study of regional and resource development in a western province. Available on order from your local library or the Government of Manitoba.

The East

The centralization of industrial growth and economic power in the metropolitan centers of Toronto and Montreal was also largely responsible for the underdevelopment of the Maritimes and most of Quebec. Studies now show, for example, that the Maritime provinces had begun to develop a viable industrial base prior to Confederation around coal, ship-building and fishing industries. Following Confederation, the Maritime industrial base began to crumble as tariff policies and freight rates favoured manufactured goods produced in central Canada and capital was directed for industrial development elsewhere. While this pattern of "development" served the industrial interests of the Montreal business elite, the rest of Quebec, particularly the rural regions where the vast majority of the French population lived, were locked into a pattern of economic underdevelopment. Indeed, the economy of Quebec was largely designed to serve the interests of the English business elite in Montreal rather than the needs of the majority of people in Quebec. In both the Atlantic provinces and Quebec, there has been a history of protest in which groups of workers, small producers, and others have struggled against these forms of exploitation and dependence.

(S) **Atlantic Regional Disparities,** Diocese of Charlottetown, Social Action Committee, 1977, 34 pages.

An historical and contemporary analysis of the regional disparities in the Maritimes. Available from Diocese of Charlottetown, Social Action Department, P.O. Box 1689, Charlottetown, P.E.I., C1A 7N4.

(S)(A) Byrd, P., **Of Dust and Times and Dreams and Agonies,** Canadian News Synthesis Project, Toronto, 1975, 150 pages.

A brief social history about the building of Canada, including a descriptive account of development in the eastern provinces. Available on order from your local bookstore.

(S) Dubuc, Alfred, **Recul de Montréal ou sous-développement du Québec?** dans **L'économie québécoise,** Rodrigue Tremblay (dir.), Presses de l'Université du Québec, Montréal, 1976, pp. 439-449.

Une analyse critique de l'état de l'économie québécoise. Disponible en bibliothèque.

(S) Gill, Louis, **Croissance et asservissement,** dans Socialisme québécois, no 23, Montréal, 1972, pp. 9-32.

Une critique du rapport Higgins-Martin-Raynauld. Disponible en bibliothèque.

(S) Higgins, B., Martin, F., Raynauld, A., **Les orientations du développement économique régional dans la province de Québec,** Rapport soumis au Ministère de l'expansion économique régionale, Ottawa, 1970.

Un rapport important sur le thème du "retard" du Québec. Disponible en bibliothèque.

Hinterland Regions

In effect, several regions of this country have been locked into a pattern of economic underdevelopment. Several factors can be noted about these hinterland regions: they provide a pool of low-wage, non-unionized labour which can be exploited by outside industries; many of the resources of these regions are exported directly to industrial centers in central Canada rather than being manufactured in the region itself and providing more jobs; in turn, they are compelled to import products required for daily life from central Canada at much higher prices; much of the industrial development in these regions is owned and controlled by outside industrial interests in collaboration with local business leaders; and the profits from the sale of resources, for the most part, are taken out of the region rather than being re-invested for the future development needs of the people. In the past decade, the federal government's programme to combat regional disparities has tended to intensify the problem. The federal strategy has been to provide large financial grants to industries willing to relocate their operations in selected "growth centers" of hinterland areas. Observers have pointed out, however, that this strategy has largely served to perpetuate disparities by favouring the economically stronger points of the region and neglecting the poorer sections; by creating employment in one part of the region that frequently results in shut-downs and layoffs in another; by making grants to large corporations for expansion, a practice which often results in hardships for small local producers.

(S) **Atlantic Regional Disparities,** Diocese of Charlottetown, Social Action Commission, 1977.

A case study of underdevelopment in a hinterland region, including an analysis of the DREE programme. Available from the Diocese of Charlottetown, Social Action Department, Charlottetown, P.E.I., C1A 7L9.

(S)(A) McGrath, D. et al., **Now That We've Burned Our Boats,** Mutual Press Ltd., Ottawa, 1978, 115 pages.

Includes an analysis of the causes of regional underdevelopment and the ineffectiveness of government programmes. (See reference above.)

(A) **Round One,** Development Education Resources Series, 1976.

A series of short popular education pamphlets concerning specific examples of underdevelopment in the Atlantic region. Available on order from the Development Education Resources Services, 1539 Birmingham St., Halifax, N.S..

(S) **The Atlantic Region of Canada: Economic Development Strategy for the 80's,** prepared by the Atlantic Development Council of Canada, St John's, Newfoundland, 1978.

A recent study of disparities and underdevelopment in the Atlantic provinces, including a strategy for the future. Available on order from the Atlantic Development Council of Canada, St John's, Newfoundland.

(A) **Une région où règne l'insécurité, le Nord-Ouest québécois,** Dossiers "vie ouvrière", no 127, Montréal, 1978.

Une série d'articles sur les conditions de vie dans une région éloignée. Disponible en s'adressant à Dossiers "vie ouvrière", 1201 rue Visitation, Montréal, H2L 3B5.

Some Christian Education-Action Projects

In some parts of Canada, Christian groups have been involved in doing research, education and action on the realities of regional underdevelopment. In Quebec, le Centre de pastorale en milieu ouvrier, for example, has both organized and participated in various education events concerning the problems and causes of underdevelopment in Quebec. The social action office in the archdiocese of Quebec has also organized seminars designed to increase critical awareness of regional and social development. In the Atlantic region, the social action co-ordinators of the Catholic dioceses have been engaged in developing a critical analysis of the underdevelopment of the Atlantic provinces. Under the sponsorship of the Atlantic bishops, this group plans to organize education-action programmes in communities throughout the region. And the Christian Institute for Social Change has recently sponsored national seminars relating to the problems of regional development and underdevelopment in Canada.

*For more information, contact: Atlantic Social Justice Committee, c/o Diocese of Charlottetown, P.O. Box 1689, Charlottetown, P.E.I. (Tel. 902-892-1251); Office de pastorale sociale, diocèse de Québec, 1073, St-Cyrille ouest, Québec, G1S 4B5 (Tel. 418-688-1211).

Some Questions For Animators

1. What are some of the principal problems of regional underdevelopment in your part of the country or province? What is the history of development and underdevelopment of your region? What is the relationship between your region and other regions of the country?

2. Are there any organizations or universities which have done studies on the development and underdevelopment of your province or region? Has your group been in contact with these studies? What have been the conclusions? What are some of the basic causes of underdevelopment of your region?

3. What critical insights can be appropriated from the Scriptures and the social teachings of the Church? What ethical or theological judgments can be made about these issues?

4. What can be done to develop more critical awareness on the part of Christians in your community concerning the problems and causes of regional underdevelopment? What methods and tools for animation purposes are useful and necessary?

5. What kind of groups or organizations are involved in trying to bring about changes in the causes of regional underdevelopment in your part of the country? What kinds of co-operation or working relationship could be developed with these organizations?

6. What are some of the common problems shared by various hinterland regions in Canada? What relevant connections can be made between the experiences of these hinterland regions and the problems of underdevelopment in Third World countries?

7. What kind of actions can be taken by Christian groups in your community to support the struggles of people trying to change the causes of general or regional underdevelopment in your part of the country?

7. Community Development

Economic and social disparities are found within each region as well as between the various regions of Canada. The problems of underdeveloped communities lie at the center of these disparities. People living in one-industry towns, neglected rural communities, or poor urban neighbourhoods are subjected to a variety of injustices. Today, many of these people find themselves involved in struggles for the very survival of their communities and their way of life.

One-Industry Towns

One-industry towns are found in the outlying regions of most provinces. The local economy of these communities is highly dependent upon one industry. This is particularly the case with mining towns. If a mining company shuts down in Sudbury, or Sydney, or Murdochville, the very survival of the community and its people is in jeopardy. Rather than developing a more diversified industrial base, including the manufacturing of resources from the mines, the community and its people are subjected to the boom and bust cycles of the mining industry. Moreover, in many small industrial towns, the social and economic development of the community is almost entirely dominated by the operations of one industry. These "company towns" are developed in such a way that the people themselves often become a captive labour force, subjected to relatively low wages and poor working conditions. The organization of workers by unions is often forbidden and the workers are highly dependent upon the benevolence of the industry. During the current period of economic recession, people living in one-industry towns are often threatened by the possibility of plant shutdowns and a struggle for the survival of their communities.

(A)   **Buchans Company Town,** Slide-tape presentation Development Education Centre, Toronto, 1978.

A look at the problems of a mining community in Newfoundland. Available on order from Development Education Centre, 121 Avenue Road, Toronto, Ontario.

(A)   **Cape Breton Steel,** GATT-Fly Project, 1976, 6 pages.

A short pamphlet illustrating some of the problems encountered in Cape Breton. Available from the GATT-Fly Project, 11 Madison Avenue, Toronto, Ontario.

(S)   Deverell, J., **Falconbridge, Portrait of a Canadian Mining Multinational,** James Lorimer Company, Toronto, 1975.

Contains a chapter on the impact of the mining industry in Sudbury. Available on order from your local bookstore.

(A)   **Quand les usines ferment,** Dossiers "vie ouvrière", no 117, Montréal, 1977.

Un numéro spécial sur les fermetures d'usines et leurs conséquences dans le milieu. Disponible à Dossiers "vie ouvrière", 1201, rue Visitation, Montréal, H2L 3B5.

(A)   **Une région où règne l'insécurité,** Dossiers "vie ouvrière", no 127, Montréal, 1978.

Une série d'articles sur les conditions de vie dans une région éloignée. Disponible en s'adressant à Dossiers "vie ouvrière", 1201 rue Visitation, Montréal, H2L 3B5.

Rural Neglect

The location of most industry in a small number of urban centers has severely restrained the possibilities of economic development in the rural areas of most provinces. In many cases, financial institutions have been reluctant to provide sufficient capital for the creation of new industries and economic opportunities. The result has been rural stagnation, declining towns, and abandoned farms. Increasingly, people in neglected rural areas are being forced to leave their homes and migrate to urban centers in search for jobs. Yet, many of the people who flock to the cities cannot find permanent jobs, end up on the welfare roles, and thereby join the ranks of the urban poor. In effect, the underdevelopment of rural or hinterland communities has been a significant cause of poverty in our cities.

(S) Banville, Charles, **Les opérations dignité,** Le fonds de recherches forestières de l'Université de Laval, Québec, 1977.

Cet ouvrage rédigé par un des pionniers des opérations dignité, décrit la mise en oeuvre d'une expérience de développement communautaire. Disponible au Fonds de recherches forestières de l'Université Laval, Université Laval, Québec, G1K 7P4.

(S)(A) **Commitment to Rural Canada, Fifth Report and Review,** Canadian Council on Rural Development, Ottawa, 1973.

A report on the need to revitalize and redevelop the rural areas. Available from the Canadian Council on Rural Development, 200 rue Principale, Place du Centre, Hull, Quebec.

(S) Hansen, N., **Rural Poverty and the Urban Crisis,** Indiana University Press, Bloomington, 1970.

An analysis of the relation between rural poverty and urban poverty. Available on order from your local bookstore.

(E) **La problématique du développement en milieu rural,** Actes du colloque tenu à l'Université du Québec à Rimouski, les 24 et 25 octobre 1975, Groupe de recherche inter-disciplinaire en développement de l'est du Québec, Université du Québec à Rimouski, Rimouski, 1976, 277 pages.

Une série de communications sur les problèmes de développement en milieu rural. Disponible en bibliothèque.

(A) **La voix du peuple,** Bulletin populaire de liaison d'Opération dignité, Matane.

Le journal-témoin du développement de l'arrière-pays et de ses habitants. On peut s'abonner en s'adressant à La voix du peuple, C.P. 91, Matane, Québec.

Urban Poverty

In most of our cities, poverty and underdevelopment are concentrated in certain neighbourhoods or communities. These underdeveloped communities are generally characterized by low tax bases, poor housing conditions, and inadequate social services. Often, the people living in these communities, provide a pool of cheap labour for certain urban industries. In recent years, these poorer neighbourhoods have been the target of urban renewal projects. Large development corporations, planning to build profitable high-rise apartments or commercial buildings have frequently concentrated on the urban land of older and poorer neighbourhoods. In many cases, land is expropriated and houses are demolished to make way for the construction of high-rise buildings. The people are uprooted and forced to seek shelter elsewhere. While the redevelopment of these communities is often necessary, the people living there are usually not given the opportunities and resources to effectively participate in the redevelopment of their own community. Instead, the land is often expropriated and redeveloped in the interests of the large development corporations and city governments. Through local community organizations and tenant unions, people in poor neighbourhoods have been able to wage a struggle for the survival of their communities and alternative forms of urban renewal in several cities.

(S)(A) **A Manual for Tenant Organizers,** NDG Tenants' Association,
Montreal, 1977, 32 pages.

Examines the problems of evictions, rent increases, reduction of services and
provides information on courses of action. Available on order from
NDG Tenants' Association, 4335 Hampton Avenue, Montreal, Quebec.

(S) **A Question of Needs,** Canadian Council for Social Development,
1975, 497 pages.

A study of people's needs (health, housing, personal social services, education,
work) in various communities across Canada. Available on order from the
Canadian Council for Social Development, 55 Parkdale Avenue,
Box 3505, Station "C", Ottawa, Ontario, K1Y 4G1.

(A) **Bleeker Street,** Development Education Centre, Toronto.

A film showing the struggle of people in a poor working-class neighbourhood
of Toronto to save their homes from a large development corporation.
Available from Development Education Centre, 121 Avenue Road,
Toronto, M5R 2G3.

(S) Gouvernement du Québec, Groupe de travail sur l'urbanisation, **L'urbanisation
au Québec,** Rapport, Direction des communications, Ministère des affaires
municipales, Québec, 1976.

Un rapport sur les problèmes de l'urbanisation visant la revalorisation du
milieu urbain. Disponible en bibliothèque.

(S) Keating, D., **The Power to Make it Happen,** Green Tree, Toronto, 1975.

An example of grass-roots community organizing in a major Canadian city.
Available on order from your local bookstore or library.

(S) Lorimer, James, **The Real World of City Politics,** Toronto, James Lewis and
Samuel, 1970, 158 pages.

A collection of case studies on urban renewal, large developers and city
politics. Available in paperback form, on order from your local bookstore.

*Voir également "Le logement échappe aux travailleurs", Dossiers "vie
ouvrière", no 103, cité dans le section **La production d'habitations.**

*Also see such references as **The Developers** and **City for Sale** in section on
housing production.

Some Christian Education-Action Programmes

In several parts of the country, Christian groups have developed education-action programmes dealing with community underdevelopment. In Cape Breton, for example, the Extension Department of St Francis Xavier University organized programmes of study and education on the problems of one-industry communities. In Quebec, citizen groups in the Saguenay and Lac Saint-Jean have created food and agricultural co-operatives based on the principle of self-reliance. Moreover, the bishops of Quebec have recently issued a statement, **Co-operation and Development,** encouraging more activity on the part of the co-operative movement. The Prairie Christian Training Center in Saskatchewan has focused attention on the problems and causes of rural underdevelopment in its programmes, which often include people from areas of rural neglect. And the Canadian Urban Training Center for Christian Mission in Toronto has organized a variety of programmes, training people to analyze and act on the problems of urban poverty. In addition, there are cases where Christian groups have been active in supporting the struggles of citizen groups in poor neighbourhoods of such cities as Toronto, Montreal, Winnipeg, Vancouver, and others.

*For more information contact: The Extension Department of St Francis Xavier University, Antigonish, Nova Scotia; Canadian Urban Training Project for Christian Mission, 51 Bond Street, Toronto, Ontario (Tel. 416-363-8944); la Fédération de Québec des Caisses populaires Desjardins, 150 avenue des Commandeurs, Lévis, Québec. For a copy of the Quebec bishops' statement **Co-operation and Development in Quebec,** contact: le Bureau des affaires sociales, Assemblée des évêques du Québec, 1225 est boul. Saint-Joseph, Montréal, Québec, H2J 1L7 (Tel. 514-272-1179).

Some Questions For Animators

1. What are some specific examples of community underdevelopment going on in your region? One-industry towns? Company towns? Rural stagnation? Urban poverty? Land expropriators? Demolition of poor neighbourhoods? Have you or your group had practical experience in educating and acting on any of these issues?

2. What kind of research or studies have been done on the specific problems of community development in your area? What have been the conclusions? Has your group done an analysis of these problems?

3. What critical insights can be appropriated from the Scriptures and the social teachings of the Church? What specific ethical or theological judgments can be made about these issues?

4. What can be done to develop more critical awareness on the part of Christian groups in your community concerning the problems of community underdevelopment in Canada? What kinds of methods or tools for animation are useful or necessary?

5. Are there any organized popular groups struggling with problems of community underdevelopment in your region? Community organizations? Tenant unions? Farmer groups? Miner unions? Citizen groups? Others? What kind of co-operation or working relationship could be developed with these groups?

6. What relevant connections can be made between the various examples of underdeveloped communities within your region? What connections or parallels exist between these communities and underdeveloped regions elsewhere in Canada? In the Third World?

7. What kinds of actions can be taken by Christian groups in your region to support people who are engaged in struggles to oppose the underdevelopment of their communities?

8. Northern Development

"We are especially concerned that the future of the North not be determined by colonial patterns of development wherein a powerful few end up controlling both the people and the resources. Some present examples of industrial planning give us cause for great concern. For what we see emerging in the Canadian North are forms of exploitation which we often assume happen only in Third World countries: a serious abuse of both the Native peoples and the energy resources of the North. Herein lies the northern dilemma: What has been described as the last frontier may become our own Third World."

(Canadian Bishops, **Northern Development: At What Cost,** *1975*)

In recent years, there has been a major shift in Canada's industrial strategies towards the development of resources in the Canadian North. The vast land mass of the North, known as the last frontier, contains valuable mineral, oil, gas, and hydro power resources. It is also the homeland of the Indian, Inuit and Métis peoples. Since time immemorial, the lands of the North have been the home and the source of livelihood for the Native people. Today, the society and culture of the northern Native peoples are being seriously threatened by large-scale industrial development projects. Through current land claims negotiations with the federal government, northern Native peoples are asserting their political rights to self-determination in the future development of the North.

Northern Territories

In the Northwest Territories and the Yukon, petroleum and mining corporations, in collaboration with the federal government are securing control over the resources of the North through the construction of drilling installations, pipelines, and mining operations. For the Native peoples, who have never surrendered their aboriginal rights to the land and its resources, rapid industrial development will have serious consequences. In the case of the Mackenzie Valley pipeline, the Berger Commission concluded that the proposed pipeline would cause serious environmental damage, resulting in economic, social and cultural underdevelopment for the Native peoples. The northern economy would be suddenly transformed to serve the industrial interests of southern Canada rather than serving the development needs of the North.

While the northern Native peoples are not against industrial development, they insist on their rights to have significant control over the future development of the North. This is imperative if development is going to serve the needs of the people in the North rather than the interests of petroleum and mining companies alone. As an alternative model, for example, the Dene in the Mackenzie Valley have proposed an economy primarily based on the development of renewable resources with controls against the rapid extraction of non-renewable resources. Similar positions have been taken by the Yukon Indians and Inuit in the Northwest Territories. So far, the federal government has resisted the basic proposals of the Native peoples for political self-determination in the future development of the Territories.

(S)   Berger, T., **Northern Frontier, Northern Homeland,** Mackenzie Valley Pipeline Inquiry Report, Vol. No. 1, Department of Supply and Services Canada, Ottawa, 1977, 213 pages.

The comprehensive study on the Native peoples and the future development of the North. Available on order from your local bookstore.

(A)   **Dene Nation,** 30 minute, 16m/m, colour film, 1979.

An audio-visual presentation of the Dene struggle for political self-determination in the North. Produced and directed by Fr. R. Fumoleau.

(S)   Fumoleau, R., **As Long as this Land Shall Last,** Toronto, McClelland and Stewart, 1973, 415 pages.

An historical analysis of Native land claims in the Mackenzie Valley. Available on order at your local bookstore.

(S) Hamelin, L.E., **Nordicité canadienne,** Hurtubise HMH, Montréal, 1975,
458 pages.

Un ouvrage très important sur le Nord canadien. Disponible en librairie.

(S) McCullum, McCullum, Olthuis, **Moratorium,** Anglican Book Centre, Toronto,
1977, 208 pages.

An analysis of the northern Native peoples' struggle against massive energy
projects and the implications for southern Canada. Available on order from
your local bookstore or library.

(S) Morisset, Jean, **Les chiens s'entre-dévorent; indiens, blancs et métis dans le
Grand Nord canadien,** Les Editions nouvelle optique, Montréal, Québec, 1977,
264 pages.

Ce livre est une version remaniée d'un rapport soumis au gouvernement du
Canada, par l'auteur, en 1975. Il traite des conséquences, des effets du
développement par les blancs chez les Amérindiens du Grand Nord canadien.
Disponible en librairie.

(S) Morisset, Jean, **Les Dénés du Mackenzie et la légitimité politique du Canada,**
dans Le Devoir du 16 octobre, 1978, pp. 5 et 6.

Morisset, Jean, **Les Dénés du Mackenzie: débat constitutionnel et permanence
autochtone,** dans Le Devoir du 17 octobre, 1978, pp. 5 et 6.

Deux articles importants sur la nature des revendications des Dénés et les
questions qu'elles posent au Canada. Disponible en bibliothèque.

(A) **Northern Development: At What Cost?,** Slide-tape presentation of the 1975
Labour Day Message of the Canadian bishops.

Available on order from Kevin Moynahan Studios, Suite 330, 144 Front Street
West, Toronto, Ontario, M5J 1G2.

(S) Watkins, M., **Dene Nation: A Colony Within,** University of Toronto Press,
Toronto, 1977, 189 pages.

A collection of studies and papers dealing with the northern economy,
particularly the Mackenzie Valley. Available at your local bookstore.

Northern Parts of the Provinces

In the northern parts of most provinces, corporations and governments are
also proceeding with plans for the industrial development of northern
resources: minerals and hydro-electric power in northern Quebec and northern
Manitoba; oil, gas, and minerals in Labrador; timber and minerals in northern
Ontario and northwest British Columbia; and uranium in northern
Saskatchewan. As is the case in the Northwest Territories and the Yukon,
these industrial development projects pose a serious threat to the future
economic development of the Native peoples in the northern regions of the
provinces. For the extraction and export of valuable non-renewable resources
from these northern regions is not geared to serve the development needs of
the Native people. In many cases, the northern economies of the provinces are
being developed, primarily to serve the industrial interests of urban centers in
the South. Moreover, with the exception of northern Quebec, these industrial
projects are proceeding either in violation of treaty rights or before there has
been a just settlement of Native land claims. As a result, these industrial
projects are bound to create forms of cultural, economic, and social
underdevelopment for the northern parts of the provinces.

(A) **Déclaration sur les droits territoriaux des autochtones,** la Commission des
droits de la personne du Québec, Montréal, 1978.

Une déclaration sur les droits territoriaux des autochtones qui se trouveront à
nouveau affectés dans un avenir rapproché par de nouveaux projets de
développement énergétique. Disponible à la Commission des droits de la
personne du Québec, 360 rue Saint-Jacques, Montréal, H2Y 1P5.

(A) **For Generations Yet Unborn,** Canadian Association in Support of Native
Peoples, Ottawa, 1977.

A collection of resource materials on industrial development in northern Ontario and the aspirations of the Native peoples. Available on order from CASNP, 904-251 Laurier Avenue West, Ottawa.

(S)   Gauquelin, M., **La Baie James pour le meilleur et le pire, I et II,** dans Québec Science, septembre et novembre 1978.

Deux articles fort bien documentés sur l'avenir de la région et des Amérindiens qui y habitent. Disponible en bibliothèque.

(S)   McCullum, H., and McCullum K., **This Land is Not For Sale,** the Anglican Book Centre, Toronto, 1975, 213 pages.

An analysis of northern development projects and native land claims in the Yukon, British Columbia, Northern Quebec, Northern Manitoba and the Mackenzie Valley. Available on order from the Anglican Book Centre, 600 Jarvis Street, Toronto, Ontario, M4Y 2J6.

(S)   **Northern Manitoba: The Project,** Canadian Association in Support of Native Peoples, Bulletin, December 1974.

A somewhat dated but still useful account of the Churchill-Nelson Hydro Project and its impact on the Native peoples of northern Manitoba. Available on order from CASNP, 904-251 Laurier Avenue West, Ottawa.

(S)   **Ontario Royal Commission on the Northern Environment, Interim Report and Recommendations,** Toronto, 1978, 39 pages.

An analysis of the environmental implications of the economic development in northern Ontario, including impact on Native peoples. Available on order from your local bookstore, or the Government of Ontario.

Southern Impact

The construction of multi-billion dollar industrial projects in the North is also expected to result in major social and economic costs for people in the southern parts of the country. In recent years, federal and provincial governments have been pouring billions of dollars of public funds into the construction of large energy projects such as the James Bay Hydro project in Quebec, the Churchill-Nelson Hydro project in northern Manitoba, and the Syncrude Tar Sands project in northern Alberta. Projects like the Alaska Highway pipeline may also place large demands on public funds. The large amount of public financing required for these projects means: that capital is drained away from other social needs like housing and social services; that less capital is available for the development of manufacturing industries which create more new jobs; that the money borrowed from foreign markets will greatly increase Canada's foreign debt. These social costs of northern energy projects will have a major impact on the poorest sectors of Canada's population. In addition, the continuous export of Canada's non-renewable energy resources and escalating energy prices raise further questions as to who benefits and who pays for these projects

(S)   **Paying the Piper,** GATT-Fly Project, 1977, 30 pages.

An important study on the economic costs involved in the construction of northern pipelines particularly for the working people of Canada. Available on order from the GATT-Fly Project, 11 Madison Avenue, Toronto.

(S)   Pratt, L., **The Tar Sands: Syncrude and the Politics of Oil,** Hurtig Publishers, Edmonton, 1976, 197 pages.

A critical and controversial study of a co-operative venture by oil companies, the federal government and the government of Alberta in the development of the Tar Sands. Available on order from your local bookstore.

(S)   **Submission to the National Energy Board Hearings on the Mackenzie Valley Pipeline,** Social Affairs Department, Canadian Conference of Catholic Bishops, 1977.

Includes an analysis of the social and economic costs of pipeline construction for southern Canada. Available at cost on order from the Publication Service, CCCB, 90 Parent Avenue, Ottawa, K1N 7B1.

Some Christian Education-Action Projects

In recent years, the Church has played an important role in developing education and action programmes in response to the injustices faced by northern Native peoples. In 1975, the Canadian bishops issued a major pastoral statement **Northern Development: At What Cost?.** In collaboration with several other Churches, they helped form Project North for the two-fold purpose of assisting northern Native organizations in communicating their struggle to people in the South and assisting Christian groups in the South to become actively involved in dealing with the ethical issues of northern development. Today, Project North has active working relationships with Native organizations and northern Church groups in the Mackenzie Valley, the Yukon, the Eastern Arctic, northern British Columbia, northern Manitoba, northern Quebec and Labrador. In addition, Christian groups in almost every province are involved in education-action programmes. Similar Church projects have also been organized to deal with problems of northern development within their province. In Saskatchewan, for example, the Inter-church Energy Coalition has focused public attention on the development of uranium resources on Native land in northern Saskatchewan through a variety of education and action programmes. And, in Quebec, le Centre Monchanin has initiated programmes on the struggles of Native peoples in northern Quebec as well as in the far North.

*For further information, contact: Project North, 154 Glenrose Avenue, Toronto, Ontario, M4T 1K8 (Tel.: 416-481-3574). Project North publishes a monthly newsletter, providing up-to-date analysis of northern development issues and information on regional activities across the country. Le Centre Monchanin, 4917 St-Urbain, Montréal, (514) 288-7229.

Some Questions For Animators:

1. What are some examples of industrial development projects in the northern parts of your province? What kind of impact are these projects having or expected to have on the Native people in the community or region? Have you or your group had some practical experience in educating and acting on these issues?

2. What kind of research or studies have been done on the problems of northern development in your province or region? What have been the conclusions? Has your group done an analysis of the injustices of northern development in your region?

3. What critical insights can be appropriated from the Scriptures and the social teachings of the Church? What specific ethical or theological judgments can be made about these issues?

4. What can be done to develop more critical awareness on the part of Christians in your community concerning the injustices of northern development? What methods and tools for animation are useful and necessary?

5. What kinds of popular groups are engaged in trying to change the patterns of industrial development in the northern parts of your province or the far North? Native peoples' organizations? Public interest groups? Environmental groups? What contact and/or working relationships could be developed with these groups?

6. What are some relevant connections between the problems of underdevelopment in the northern regions of your province and other examples of regional underdevelopment? Urban renewal projects? The Maritimes? The Northwest Territories? What are some of the connections between these problems and those of the Third World?

7. What kinds of actions can be taken by Christian groups in your region to support the struggles of Native people and other groups striving to change exploitative patterns of development in the northern parts of your province?

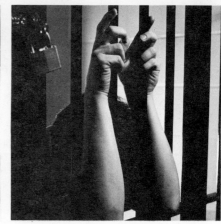

9. Consumer Society

"Industrial strategies are designed specifically to produce maximum gratification and profit, so that wasteful consumption is systematically promoted. In the process, both human beings and natural resources are being abused or destroyed."
Canadian Bishops, **A Society to be Transformed,** *1977.*

In our industrial society, a high priority has been placed on the production and consumption of luxury goods. This has lead to the creation of a consumer-oriented society whose priorities are largely determined by the production of luxury goods rather than serving basic human needs. Today, people are raising serious questions about the deteriorating quality of life that has resulted from this pattern of production and consumption.

Luxury Production and Consumption

In our society, it is clear that the production system is primarily organized around the goal of maximizing profits and growth. To maximize their profits, industries have put increasing priority on the production of luxury goods rather than providing the basic necessities of life. As a result, our society produces tons of frivolous goods — e.g. colour televisions, cosmetics of all kinds, quiet-ride cars, etc. — but cannot provide the basic needs of life — adequate food, clothing, shelter, employment, energy — for close to a quarter of Canada's population. In order to create markets for the sale of their luxury products, industries have systematically promoted patterns of luxury consumption. Through relentless advertizing, people are made to believe that luxury, non-essential goods are necessary for a happy life. Moreover, this pattern of production results in a serious waste of resources that could be developed to serve the vital needs of people in our society and elsewhere in the world.

(S)(A) **Abondance et gaspillage,** Programme Chantier, Office de catéchèse du Québec, Montréal, 1979.

Un document d'information et de reflexion sur la société de consommation. Disponible à l'Office de catéchèse du Québec, 2715 Chemin Côte Sainte-Catherine, Montréal. H3T 1B6.

(S) **Canada as a Conserver Society,** Science Council of Canada, Ottawa, 1977.

A critical study of our consumer-oriented society in Canada and the prospects of creating a society based on conservation. Available on order from the Science Council of Canada, 150 Kent Street, Ottawa, K1P 5P4.

(S) Commoner, B., **The Poverty of Power,** Bantram Books Edition, New York, 1977, 297 pages.

An important critical analysis of the production-consumption cycle and its impact on our society. Available on order from your local bookstore.

(S)(A) **La Consommation,** Programme Chantier, Office de catéchèse du Québec, Montréal, 1974.

Un dossier de réflexion et de références documentaires. Disponible à l'Office de catéchèse du Québec, 2715 chemin Côte Sainte-Catherine, Montréal, Québec, H3T 1B6.

(S)(A) Valaskakis, K., and others, **The Selective Conserver Society.**

A popular version of research prepared for the federal government, that analyzes the implications of a conserver society. Available on order from your local bookstore.

Social Breakdown

The pattern of luxury production and consumption has had a significant social and cultural impact on the quality of life in our society. The advertizing programmes of corporations have introduced a whole set of material values and expectations which largely shape people's attitudes today about the "good life". The increasing dependency on credit cards, "buy now pay later" plans, and non-durable products has greatly affected the attitudes and habits of people in our society. Indeed, many people are caught in the trappings of a consumer throw-away society. Trapped in the credit card syndrome, large numbers of people have fallen into serious personal debt. At the same time, the realities of social breakdown today — family break-ups, separations and divorces, the increasing use of alcohol and drugs, and the rising numbers of crimes, suicides, and murders — have been largely influenced by the priorities and values generated in our consumer society. Moreover, there is growing evidence that these realities of social breakdown are intensifying in the more affluent communities.

(A) **Consumer Credit: A Blessing or a Curse,** Institute for Saskatchewan Studies, Saskatoon, 1978.

A newsletter that discusses the problems of personal debt in our consumer society. Available on order from the Institute for Saskatchewan Studies, Box 1462, Saskatoon, Sask., S7N 3P7.

(S) Dumont, R., **L'utopie ou la mort,** Paris, Seuil, collection "politique", 1974, 186 pages.

Un livre sur les problèmes posés par la société de consommation à l'échelle mondiale. Disponible en librairie.

(S) Illich, I., **Tools for Conviviality,** New York, Harper and Row, 1973.

A critical analysis of the modern society engulfed by consumerism. Available on order from your local bookstore.

(S) **Le droit de vivre sans s'endetter,** Manifeste du Mouvement ACEF du Québec, Montréal, mai 1978.

Ce document se veut un outil d'information et de revendications destiné à la population pour qu'elle bénéficie des acquis du mouvement ACEF dans sa lutte contre l'endettement. Disponible à la Fédération des ACEF, 1212 rue Panet, Montréal, Québec.

Environmental Damage

The pattern of luxury production and consumption has also had a detrimental impact on the environment. Changes in production technology, designed to maximize efficiency and profits, have posed serious threats to the environment in recent years. Plastics have replaced wood, synthetic fibres have replaced natural fibres, detergents have replaced natural soaps, chemicals have replaced organic materials — all of which are pollution-causing materials that have a damaging effect on the air, lakes, rivers and waters. In effect, these new production technologies have posed a threat to the balance of creation itself. While federal, provincial and municipal governments have imposed pollution controls on some industries, these controls have seldom been sufficient or strictly enforced. Moreover, the new production technologies require a great deal of natural gas and oil. As a result, industries have placed enormous demands on non-renewable supplies of oil and gas, thus contributing to energy shortages.

(S)   Commoner, B., **The Closing Circle,** Bantam Book Edition, New York, 1974, 343 pages.

Â study that shows the impact of industrial production, consumption and environmental damage. Available on order from your local bookstore.

(S)   Commoner, B., **Science for Survival,** The Viking Press, New York, 1967, 150 pages.

This book analyzes the vast forces unleashed by science without knowledge of what long-range effects on the environment will be. Available on order from your local bookstore.

(S)(A)   Gouvernement du Québec, **Environnement-Education,** Service de protection de l'environnement, Editeur officiel, Québec, 1978.

Un recueil de textes pour la réflexion et la discussion sur le thème de l'éducation mésologique. Disponible à Environnement-Education, 207 est Crémazie, 3 ième étage, Montréal, Québec, H2M 1L2.

(S)   Samuel, P., **Ecologie: détente ou cycle infernal,** Union générale d'éditions, Paris, 1973, 445 pages.

Un examen critique du gaspillage généralisé suivi de propositions pour y remédier. Disponible en librairie.

Some Christian Education-Action Programmes

In recent years, a variety of Christian groups across the country have initiated education and action programmes dealing with the problems of luxury production and consumption. In Quebec, for example, the Chantier programme recently devoted a full year of its education activities to increasing critical awareness concerning the problems of our consumer society in parishes. Other education programmes, on a much smaller scale, have been initiated elsewhere in Canada. The creation of small Christian communities, in which people attempt to develop alternative lifestyles in contrast to the values and priorities of our consumer society, has also been a significant response. In addition, some groups have been directly engaged in dealing with the problems of environmental damage or social breakdown.

*For further information, contact: Chantiers, Office de la catéchèse du Québec, 2715 Côte Sainte-Catherine, Montréal, H3T 1B6 (Tel.: 514-735-5751); la Fédération des ACEF, 1212 rue Panet, Montréal, Québec (Tel.: 514-526-0823).

Some Questions For Animators:

1. What are some of the major problems concerning luxury production and consumption in your region or community? What kinds of luxury, non-essential goods are being produced? What impact do advertizing schemes have in determining patterns of luxury consumption and life-styles of people in your community?

2. What are some examples of pollution or environmental damage in your region? What are some examples of social breakdown? What do these problems tell us about the quality of life being generated in our society?

3. What kinds of research or studies have been done on these issues in your community or region? What have been the conclusions? What experience has your group had in educating and acting on these problems?

4. What critical insights can be appropriated from the Scriptures and the social teachings of the Church? What specific ethical or judgments can be made about these issues?

5. What kinds of groups are actively engaged in trying to change the problems and causes of our consumer society? Environmental groups? Conserver society groups? What kind of co-operation or working relationships can be established with these groups?

6. What can be done to increase critical awareness among Christians in your community or region concerning the problems of a society based on patterns of luxury production and consumption? What kinds of animation methods and tools are necessary and useful?

7. What relevant connections can be made between the problems of luxury production and consumption in our society and that of Third World countries?

8. What kinds of actions can be taken by Christian groups in your community or region to support people attempting to free themselves from the trappings of our consumer society?

10. Minority Discrimination

"We deem it timely to recall the firm declaration of John XXIII: 'It is our duty to state most explicitly, that every policy which tends to block the life and growth of minority groups is a grave crime against justice, and graver still when its aim is to wipe out such minorities. On the other hand, nothing is more in harmony with justice than any line of action which aims at a better life for ethnic minorities, especially, as it concerns their language, culture, customs, resources and economic enterprises' ".

Canadian Bishops, **Letter on the 100th Anniversary of Confederation,** *1967. Quote from John XXIII,* **Pacem in Terris,** *1963.*

It is often said that a test of any developed or civilized society is how well it treats its own minority groups. Yet, throughout the building of our industrial society, minority groups have experienced forms of discrimination and even repression. Today, various forms of cultural, racial and sexual discrimination are built into the social and economic institutions of our society. Indeed, it has been stated that if you are a woman or a native Indian or a francophone person, your chances of being poor in Canada are much greater than if you are young, white, male and English-speaking.

Cultural Discrimination

Throughout Canada's history, francophone minorities have had to face forms of cultural domination and discrimination. The federal government's Bilingualism and Biculturalism Report for example, clearly documented that the English language has been the dominant language of economic life in Quebec and that the average income of either unilingual French or bilingual workers was much less than that of unilingual English. At the same time, francophone minorities living and working in the other provinces have virtually found it impossible to maintain the existence of their own language and cultural heritage. While some changes in attitudes towards francophone minorities have occurred over the past decade, the forces of cultural assimilation into the dominant English-speaking society remain very strong. Other cultural minorities, especially Native peoples, have suffered similar forms of cultural domination. In recent times, these minorities have begun to organize against forms of domination and assimilation in different regions of the country for the protection of their rights and to exercise more self-determination over their economic, political and cultural affairs.

(S) **Francophones hors Québec,** numéro special de Relations, avril 1978, no 436.

Une série d'articles sur l'avenir des communautés francophones hors Québec. Disponible en bibliothèque.

(S) **The Heirs of Lord Durham,** translated by the Canadian Council of Christians and Jews, Toronto, 1978.

A translation of an important study done by the Fédération des francophones hors Québec on the situation of the French minorities in English Canada. Available on order from the Burna and Mackachern, Suite 3, 62 Railside Road, Don Mills, Ontario.

(S) La Fédération des francophones hors Québec, **Deux poids deux mesures. Les francophones hors Québec et les anglophones au Québec: un dossier comparatif,** Ottawa, 1978, 63 pages.

Une analyse comparative de la situation des francophones hors Québec et des anglophones du Québec. Disponible en écrivant à la Fédération des francophones hors Québec, 1, rue Nicholas, Suite 1404, Ottawa, Ontario, K1N 7B6.

Racial Discrimination

The treatment of the Native peoples of Canada constitutes the primary example of racial domination and discrimination in the building of our industrial society. Today, Indian, Métis and Inuit peoples generally occupy a position at the bottom of our economic life, still subject to discrimination in the work place, in schools, and society at large. In terms of their population, they experience the highest rates of unemployment, alcoholism, suicide, and infant mortality. In addition to Native people, immigrants from Africa, the Carribean, Asia, and Latin America are confronted with racial discrimination in employment, housing and schools. In these times of economic recession, racial minorities who have emigrated from other countries for economic reasons, often become the scapegoat for unemployment and related problems. As a result, racial tensions are mounting in our cities.

(S) Cardinal, H., **The Unjust Society: The Tragedy of Canada's Indians,** Hurtig Co., Edmonton, 1969.

A critical review of the plight of Indian people in Canada. Available on order from your local bookstore.

(A) Hill, D.G., **Human Rights in Canada: Focus on Racism,** Canadian Labour Congress, Ottawa, 1977, 40 pages.

A basic book on racism in Canada. Available by writing the Community Programme Service, Canadian Labour Congress, 2841 Riverside Drive, Ottawa.

(S) Howard, J., **Strange Empire, Louis Riel and the Métis People,** Lewis and Samuel, Toronto, 1974, 601 pages.

A biography of Louis Riel and the history of the Métis people in Manitoba and Saskatchewan. Available on order from your local bookstore.

Sexual Discrimination

In spite of expressed concerns for women's equality in our society, women continue to experience various forms of discrimination. The Royal Commission on the Status of Women concluded that women in all types of work earned less than men, and educational qualifications were worth less to women than to men. Today, the average working woman still earns only half as much income as working men and receives little or no job protection. At the same time, homosexual men and women are being faced with discrimination in jobs and housing. Indeed, many people of homosexual orientation, men and women, experience fear and loneliness in their daily lives. In recent years, women and homosexuals have been organizing to protect their rights and to develop greater public awareness on the problems they face in society today.

(A) **Dignity,** Dignity/Canada, Calgary, Alberta, 1978.

A pamphlet outlining the goals, analysis, and action of Dignity/Canada, a Catholic homophile organization in Canada. Available on order from Dignity/Canada, P.O. Box 1492, Station T, Calgary, Alberta, T2N 2H7.

(S) Gouvernement du Québec, Conseil du statut de la femme, **Pour les Québécoises: égalité et indépendance,** Editeur officiel du Québec, Québec, 1978, 335 pages.

Un document qui propose une politique d'ensemble concernant la condition féminine. Disponible en librairie.

(A) **La lutte des femmes, combat de tous les travailleurs,** dans Présence chrétienne au monde ouvrier, Mouvement des travailleurs chrétiens, Montréal, juin 1978, no 71, 19 pages.

Un examen de la question, par les femmes de la classe ouvrière. Disponible au Mouvement des travailleurs chrétiens, 7559 boul. St-Laurent, Montréal, Québec.

(S) Reuther, R., **New Woman: New Earth,** Seabury Press, New York, 1975.

An example of theological reflection on women and their struggle for justice. Available on order from your local bookstore or library.

(S) **Women in Need: A Source Book,** Canadian Council for Social Development, 1977.

Examines the problems of low-income women in relation to housing, health care, day care services and legal services. Available on order from the Canadian Council of Social Development, 55 Parkdale Avenue, Box 3505, Station "C", Ottawa, Ontario, K1Y 4G1.

(A) **Women Working,** Issue No. 6, United Church of Canada Publication, Toronto, 1975, 8 pages.

A general introduction to the problems of working women. Available from the United Church of Canada, 85 St Clair Avenue East, Toronto, Ontario.

*See Dossiers "vie ouvrière", **Les ouvrières du vêtement,** in the industrial exploitation section.

Social Outcasts

In addition to cultural, racial and sexual discrimination, some minority groups tend to be treated as social outcasts by the larger society. Elderly people, no longer considered useful to society, are frequently confined to rest homes or compelled to live out the rest of their lives on inadequate pensions. Prisoners, most of whom come from the poorer sectors of society, are often subjected to inhumane conditions in our penitentiaries and discrimination in finding jobs once they are released. And the mentally or physically handicapped, often considered to be the "untouchables" of our society, are separated from the rest of the population in institutions.

(A) **Alternatives,** Church Council for Justice and Corrections, Montreal, 1976.

A guide for study and action on the problems of the criminal justice system in Canada. Available on order from the Church Council on Justice and Corrections, 200 boul. Davignon, Cowansville, Quebec, J2K 1N9.

(S)(A) **The Aging in Canada,** National Council of Welfare, Ottawa, 1966, 36 pages.

A report on the aging in Canada. Available by writing to the National Council of Welfare, Brooke Claxton Building, Ottawa, Ontario, K1A 0K9.

(S) **Housing the Elderly,** Canadian Council for Social Development, Ottawa, 1976, 175 pages.

A report on the housing problems encountered by elderly people in Canada. Available from the Canadian Council for Social Development, 55 Parkdale Avenue, Box 3505, Station "C", Ottawa, Ontario, K1Y 4G1.

(A) **The Injustice of It All,** Issue No. 17, United Church of Canada Publication, Toronto, 1977, 6 pages.

A critical analysis of the Canadian criminal justice system. Available from United Church of Canada, 85 St Clair Avenue East, Toronto, Ontario.

(A) **The Old Ones,** Development Education Centre, Toronto, 1977.

A slide-tape montage which compares the experience of growing old in Canada with that of China. Available on order from the Development Education Centre, 121 Avenue Road, Toronto, Ontario.

(S) **Personal Social Services for the Handicapped,** Canadian Council for Social Development, Ottawa, Ontario, 1977.

A report analyzing the provision of personal social services for the physically handicapped, the mentally retarded and the mentally ill in each province. Available on order from the Canadian Council for Social Development, 55 Parkdale Avenue, Box 3505, Station "C", Ottawa, Ontario, K1Y 4G1.

(S)(A) Vanier, J, **Eruption to Hope,** Griffin House Publishers, Toronto, 1971, 105 pages.

Provides deep insights concerning the plight and the aspirations of the mentally and physically handicapped. Available on order from you local bookstore.

Some Christian Education-Action Programmes

In the Church today, there are a variety of education and action projects dealing with the discrimination of minority groups. For the most part, these programmes are organized in dioceses. In the western provinces for example, several dioceses have pastoral programmes which are, in part, designed to combat racial discrimination affecting Native peoples, particularly in cities. In Ontario, the Canadian Religious Conference has organized an education programme dealing with the problems of cultural discrimination, particularly concerning francophone minorities. In Québec, l'Association féminine d'éducation et d'action sociale has developed programmes to increase the awareness of women's rights in society and the Church. At the same time, there are several national organizations in the Church dealing with specific problems of minority groups: l'Arche projects concerning the mentally and physically handicapped exist in several communities of the country; Dignity has been formed to assist homosexuals in the recognition of the rights; and the Church Council on Justice and Corrections has sponsored a country-wide educational programme concerning the conditions of prisoners in penitentiaries.

*For further information, contact: Fédération des francophones hors Québec, 1 rue Nicholas, suite 1404, Ottawa, Ontario, K1N 7B6 (Tel.: 613-563-0311); Association féminine d'éducation et d'action sociale, 180 rue Dorchester est, Montréal, Québec (Tel.: 514-866-1863); Church Council on Justice and Corrections, 200 boul. Davignon, Cowansville, Québec, J2N 1N9 (Tel.: 514-263-3073).

Some Questions For Animators:

1. What are some specific examples of minority discrimination in your community or region? Cultural discrimination? Racial discrimination? Sexual discrimination? Other forms of social discrimination? Have you or your group had some practical experience in educating and acting on any of these issues?

2. What kind of research or studies have been done on specific problems of minority discrimination in your community or region? What have been the conclusions? Has your group done an analysis of these problems?

3. What critical insights can be found in the Scriptures or the social teachings? What specific ethical or theological judgments can be made about minority discrimination?

4. What can be done to develop a critical awareness among Christians in your community on the problems and causes of minority discrimination? What kinds of animation methods and tools are necessary and useful?

5. What kind of minority groups are active in your community to protect their rights? Francophone groups? Native peoples' groups? Black organizations? Women's groups? Elderly groups? Handicapped communities? Other minority groups? What kind of co-operation or working relationship could be established with these organizations?

6. What relevant connections can be made between the injustices of minority discrimination here in Canada and the repression of minority groups in the Third World and eastern European countries? What are some of the similarities and differences?

7. What kinds of actions can be taken by Christian groups to support the struggles of specific minority groups in your region?

11. Social Control

"...the redistribution of wealth, not the control or exclusion of people, is the long-range goal towards which we should aim in building the kind of future society we want."
(Canadian Bishops, **Brief to the Special Parliamentary Committee on Immigration)**

In recent years, a series of regulations have been introduced by governments to control the activities and movements of people in our society. Increased security measures and police surveillance plus stricter immigration laws and tighter controls on public information are examples of this trend. In times of economic uncertainty, there is a tendency for governments to put tighter controls on the activities of people in order to curb social unrest. Yet, such controls contribute to an erosion of civil liberties and raise serious questions about the future of democratic rights in our society.

National Security

There are signs of growing preoccupation with "national security" in Canada today. In order to provide a stable climate for foreign investment and economic growth, governments are compelled to curb social unrest, particularly in these times of economic uncertainty. In Canada, the Keable Commission and the MacDonald Commission have recently revealed evidence about increasing intervention of police and security forces in the lives and activities of people. A variety of labour unions, immigrants, refugees, universities, political groups, church groups, civic and community associations have become targets of police surveillance in our society. The recent wire tapping legislation and proposed legislation on mail opening are designed to increase police powers for surveillance. Yet, it has also become evident that police have been engaged in illegal surveillance operations. "National security" or "national interest" are frequently used to justify these activities.

(S) Caron, N., et alii, **La police secrète au Québec,** Editions Québec/Amérique, Montréal, 1978, 228 pages.

Une série d'articles sur les agissements de la police au Québec et au Canada. Disponible en librairie.

(S) Fernandez, A., **La doctrine de la sécurité nationale,** dans Projet, no 128, pp. 973-985.

Un exposé portant sur l'origine et l'application de la doctrine de la sécurité nationale ainsi que sur ses conséquences socio-économiques. Disponible en bibliothèque.

(S) **Mounting Repression: Its meaning and importance for Quebec and Canada,** la Ligue des droits de l'homme, Montréal, 1978.

An analysis of the current economic crisis and the repression of civil liberties in Quebec and Canada. Available on order from la Ligue des droits de l'homme, 3836 St-Hubert, Montréal, Québec, H2L 4A5.

(S)(A) **Un dossier noir sur la police politique,** la Ligue des droits de l'homme, Montréal, 1978, 16 pages.

Une étude sur les activités de la police politique. Disponible à la Ligue des droits de l'homme, 3826 St-Hubert, Montréal, Québec, H2L 4A5.

(S)(A) **Vers un Etat policier, les dessous de la sécurité nationale,** Montréal, dans Opération liberté, Vol. 1, no 2, la Ligue des droits de l'homme, avril 1978, 23 pages.

Résumé des implications réelles des activités de la police au Québec et au Canada. Disponible à la Ligue des droits de l'homme, 3826 St-Hubert, Montréal, Québec, H2L 4A5.

Immigration Controls

Canada's new immigration legislation provides another example of policies designed to control people in times of economic uncertainty. The new legislation outlines stringent controls to regulate the number of immigrants to Canada. The primary reason for these new controls is that too many people cause or aggravate our economic problems. Indeed, immigration is used as a tool for economic planning by governments and stricter immigration controls are introduced in times of economic uncertainty. At the same time, there is growing evidence that refugees from repressive regimes are experiencing forms of harassment here in Canada. Increasingly, refugees are subjected to tight screenings, lengthy police interrogations, and are even placed under surveillance by domestic security forces after visas are granted. While some security measures may be necessary, there is a danger that they may become excessive.

(S)(A) **Immigration (Proposed Changes in the Immigration Bill),** Inter-church Project on Population et alii, Ottawa, 1977.

A critical analysis of the Immigration Bill by several inter-church projects. While somewhat outdated, the basic points made here are still relevant. Available at cost from the Inter-Church Project on Population, c/o Publication Service, CCCB, 90 Parent Avenue, Ottawa, Ontario, K1N 7B1.

(A) **The Immigrant Worker,** Organization to Fight for the Democratic Rights of Immigrants, Montreal, 1978.

A newspaper oriented towards protecting the democratic rights of immigrants. Available on order from the OFDRI, Box 636, Station "H", Montréal, H3G 2M6.

(S) **Mémoire concernant le Bill C-24,** Ligue des droits de l'homme, Montréal, juin 1977, 51 pages.

Une analyse critique (faite par des groupes et des individus) commanditée par la Ligue et présentée au Comité permanent sur le travail, la main-d'oeuvre et l'immigration.

(A) **The Politics of People,** Issue No. 9, United Church of Canada Publication, Toronto, 1975, 8 pages.

An overview of immigration issues, including refugee policies. Available from the United Church of Canada, 85 St Clair Avenue East, Toronto.

Control of Information

In Canada today, governments and corporations exercise a great deal of control over information on public matters affecting the lives of people. Information, vital to discussion and debate on matters of public policy, is often kept secret. While there are valid reasons for withholding certain information, freedom of information is an important democratic right. Yet, by controlling access to adequate information, governments and corporations are able to control the activities of people who wish to bring about social change. Moreover, the major news networks (newspapers, radio, television) which are concentrated in the hands of a small number of large corporations, exercise considerable control through their power to be selective on what information is made public.

(S) **De la précarité de la presse ou le citoyen menacé,** rapport du Comité de travail sur la concentration de la presse écrite, Québec, 1977.

Une étude sur le phénomène de la concentration économique dans le secteur de la presse écrite. Disponible gratuitement à tout bureau de Communications Québec.

(A) **Freedom of Information vs. Government Secrecy.** The Ontario Public Interest Group, Waterloo, Ontario, 1977, 8 pages.

A critical review of the freedom of information legislation in Canada and the secrecy of governmental actions. Available on order from OPIRG, c/o University of Waterloo, Ontario.

(A) **Le pouvoir de l'information,** 1) expérience et lutte, 2) bilan et prospective, Dossiers "vie ouvrière", nos 125 et 126, Montréal, 1977.

Deux numéros consacrés à l'information et aux moyens d'information. Disponibles à Dossiers "vie ouvrière", 1201 rue Visitation, Montréal, H2L 3B5.

(S) **Who Calls the Tune.** Canadian Council on Social Development, Ottawa, 1977.

A publication recounting the experiences of small community organizations with the media. Available on order from the Canadian Council on Social Development, 55 Parkdale Avenue, Box 3505, Station "C", Ottawa, K1Y 4G7.

Law and Order

The current trend towards control of people is reinforced by feelings of fear and an increasing concern for "law and order". Surveys show that public attitudes towards crime in the streets, capital punishment, and the prison system itself, are hardening. Very often the victims are the poor and the disadvantaged in our society. Indeed, there is a vital connection between crime and poverty, and a disproportionate number of people in our prisons today come from poorer families.

(A) **The Injustice of it All ...** Issue No. 17, United Church of Canada Publication, Toronto, November 1977, 6 pages.

A critical evaluation of the criminal justice system in Canada including the relationship between crime and poverty. Available from the United Church of Canada, 85 St Clair Avenue East, Toronto, Ontario.

(S) Eglise unie du Canada, **La prison, un chaînon du cycle criminel,** dans l'Eglise canadienne, vol. xii, no 9, 14 décembre 1978, pp. 239-242.

Une brève réflexion sur le système judiciaire. Disponible en bibliothèque.

(S) Eglise unie du Canada, **Le code criminel et les crimes,** dans l'Eglise canadienne, vol. xii, no 7, 30 novembre 1978, pp. 199-202.

Une courte réflexion sur le code criminel et le système judiciaire. Disponible en bibliothèque.

Some Christian Education-Action Projects

Increasing awareness of social controls and the possible erosion of democratic rights have given rise to several education and action projects. In Quebec, la Ligue des droits de l'homme has done research on the phenomenon of national security in Canada, conducted education programmes on the problems of increasing police powers, and initiated actions for changes in government policies. The Inter-church Project on Population in collaboration with the Inter-church Committee on Human Rights in Latin America and other groups were engaged in organizing a campaign to bring about specific changes in the immigration legislation before its final passage in Parliament. And the Church Council on Justice and Corrections has sponsored a nation-wide education programme designed, in part, to change public attitudes towards "law and order" and the criminal justice system in Canada.

*For further information, contact: la Ligue des droits de l'homme, 3826 St-Hubert, Montréal, Québec, H2L 4A5 (Tel.: 514-844-2815); Inter-church Project on Population, c/o 90 Parent Avenue, Ottawa, Ontario, K1N 7B1 (Tel.: 613-236-9461, ext. 249).

Some Questions For Animators:

1. What are some specific examples of social controls in your own region or community? Police surveillance? Control of public information? Surveillance of refugees? What kind of public attitudes exist towards law and order? Have you or your group had any practical experience with these problems?

2. What kinds of research or studies have been done on any of these problems in your community or region? What have been the conclusions? Has your group done an analysis of these problems?

3. What critical insights can be appropriated from the Scriptures and the social teachings of the Church? What specific ethical or theological judgments can be made about these issues?

4. What can be done to develop a critical awareness among Christians in your community or region concerning the problems of social control and erosion of democratic rights? What kinds of animation methods and tools are necessary and useful?

5. What kinds of public interest groups in your region are stimulating public awareness concerning the problems of social control? Human Rights groups? Civil liberties associations? What kinds of co-operation or working relationships can be developed with these organizations?

6. What relevant connections can be made between the problems of social controls and erosion of democratic rights in Canada and the hard realities of repressive regimes in most Third World countries? What are some of the similarities and differences?

7. What kinds of actions can be taken by Christian groups in your community or region to support public interest groups struggling for the preservation of civil liberties and democratic rights?

JUSTICE
IN THE
THIRD WORLD

Introduction

In Canada, various parts of the Christian community have been developing a critical awareness of the problems of poverty and oppression in the Third World. The Canadian Catholic Organization for Development and Peace, for example, has coordinated an extensive education programme in Christian communities throughout Canada on the realities of underdevelopment in the Third World. At the same time, a variety of other Christian groups and action-research projects have been evolving a critical analysis of Canada's relationship to the Third World on specific problems of injustice.

This chapter is a working paper for Christian animators concerned about the problems of social and economic injustice in the poor countries of the Third World. It is designed to stimulate a critical awareness of Canada's role in relation to the underdevelopment of the Third World. The objectives are four-fold: (i) to briefly identify and comment on some of the problems and causes of underdevelopment in the Third World; (ii) to list some resource materials which may be useful for study and animation; (iii) to identify some Christian education and action programmes on specific issues; (iv) to pose some questions for reflection on the part of Christian animators.

The central theme of this chapter concerns another side of the "Canadian paradox". On the one hand, Canada has many of the characteristics of an underdeveloped country and therefore has some common links with the problems faced by Third World countries today (see chapter No. 2, Justice in Canada, for discussion of this point). On the other hand, Canada participates as an industrialized country in the global economy, and thereby plays a role in the exploitation of Third World countries. This is the paradox that underlies our discussion in this chapter concerning Canada's relationship to the underdevelopment of the Third World today.

This working paper is divided into ten sections dealing with the following topics: (1) Underdevelopment of the Third World; (2) The Global Economy; (3) Self-Reliant Development; (4) Foreign Aid; (5) International Trade; (6) Foreign Investment; (7) World Hunger; (8) Repression of Human Rights; (9) Military Armament; (10) Immigration. Each of these sections may be treated as a separate unit for study and reflection by animators, recognizing that there are internal relationships between the various topics and sections.

Several limitations should be noted. First, this working paper is limited to a discussion of injustices in the Third World and does not take up the problems of injustices found in many other parts of the world. The repression of human rights in the Soviet Union and eastern European countries is a case in point. This chapter, therefore, is somewhat limited in scope, as far as global injustices are concerned. Second, the list of resource materials is neither complete nor comprehensive. Most of the resource materials listed have been selected because they are helpful in stimulating a more critical awareness of the problems and causes of injustice in the Third World today. Yet, these diverse materials may also present contradictory points of view. Thus, it is important to recognize that these resource materials do not necessarily represent the position or policy of the bishops on the various topics under discussion. They are presented for the information of animators.*

Finally, it should be understood again that this is a "working" instrument for animators. For this very reason, this document is incomplete. It proposes a framework for Christians to develop critical awareness and action on the issues of injustice in Canada's relationship to the Third World. Animators are encouraged to adopt this instrument in relation to the particular needs of their groups. At the same time, this working instrument requires further refinement and completion by animators engaged in developing education and action on these and related issues.

*Most of the resources in this chapter are listed in alphabethical order Those which are directly useful for animation purposes are identified by (A) and those which are more useful for study purposes are identified by (S).

General References

It is, of course, impossible to identify all the relevant data and resource materials concerning specific problems of justice in Canada's relations to the Third World. In addition to more specific references listed in this working paper, there are some general references that may be useful for animators.

a) Development and Peace publishes two monthly newspapers (one English, one French) that provide some current information on issues of justice in the Third World and the work of the Church;

Global Village Voice: available on order from Development and Peace, 67 Bond Street, Toronto, Ontario.

Solidarités: disponible à Développement et Paix, 2111 rue Centre, Montréal, Québec.

b) There are several regular sources for documentation on issues of justice pertaining to the Third World. For example:

New Internationalist: a monthly periodical providing current information and analysis on issues of World development (available on order from New Internationalist, 113 Atlantic Avenue, Brooklyn, New York, 11201.

IDOC: International Documentation and Communication Centre provides information on documents and research concerning issues of World development and the activities of Churches (for the IDOC catalogue, write to IDOC International, Via S. Maria dell,Anima, 30, 00186, ROMA).

c) Audio-Visual Catalogues: films and slide-tape presentations useful for animation purposes, are available.

—Development and Peace has a small library of films and audio-visuals on Third World issues. For a film list, contact: the Education Co-ordinator, Development and Peace, 67 Bond Street, Toronto, Ontario.

—Canadian Council for International Co-operation has a library of 1,300 films. For a film catalogue, contact: Canadian Council for International Co-operation, 321 Chapel Street, Ottawa, Ontario, K1N 2Z2.

—Catalogue de références des audio-visuels sur le sous-développement et le développement, produced by Carrefour d'information Québec-intermonde, 1650 Ozias-Leduc, Mont St-Hilaire, Québec.

d) The National Conference of the Bishops of Brazil have sponsored a world-wide education-action programme called International Study Days for a Society Overcoming Dominations. Case studies, outlining various struggles for justice around the world, have been compiled in a document entitled, **A Society Overcoming Dominations.** Available on order from International Study Days, Box 661, San Francisco, CA 94101.

I. Underdevelopment of the Third World

"It must certainly be recognized that colonizing powers have often furthered their own interests, power or glory, and that their departure has sometimes left a precarious economy, bound up for instance with production of one kind of crop whose market prices are subject to sudden and considerable variation."
(Paul VI, **Populorum Progressio,** No. 7, 1967)

"We refer here, particularly, to the implications for our countries of dependence on a center of economic power around which they gravitate. For this reason our nations frequently do not own their goods, or have a say in economic decisions affecting them. It is obvious that this will not fail to have political consequences given the interdependence of these two fields."
(Latin American Bishops, **Medellin Documents,** Peace, No. 8, 1968)

The countries of Asia, Africa and Latin America, comprising two thirds of this planet, are generally referred to as the Third World. The vast majority of people in these countries today suffer from conditions of poverty, oppression, and misery. For centuries, the peoples of the Third World have been subjugated to various forms of underdevelopment — economic, political, cultural and social.

Colonial Roots

The present realities of poverty, oppression and underdevelopment in Third World countries are rooted in the colonialism of previous centuries. In the period between the sixteenth and the nineteenth centuries, Africa, Asia, and Latin America were carved up into numerous colonies for the primary purpose of supplying raw materials to the emerging industrial nations of Europe. Through this process, the industrialized countries accumulated enormous wealth but the economies of Third World countries were seriously distorted and fractured in the process. Valuable resources such as food-producing land, raw materials, and human energies were directed away from local development needs to produce products required by the industrialized countries. This left the economies of the Third World in a fragile state of dependence and uneven growth, not able to provide for the basic needs of their own people. And, along with this economic underdevelopment, there have been a variety of social and cultural injustices for the peoples of the Third World.

(S)   **Africa Speaks,** Development Education Centre, 1973, Toronto.

A collection of articles and papers on the problems of underdevelopment in Africa, historically and in the present. Available from Development Education Centre, 121 Avenue Road, Toronto, M5R 2G3.

(S) Bairoch, P., **Le tiers monde dans l'impasse,** Paris, Gallimard, coll. idées, 1971, 372 pages.

Un historique de l'évolution de l'Occident et une analyse des origines de l'évolution et des causes du sous-développement économique. Disponible en librairie.

(S) Bigo, P., **The Church and-the Third World Revolution,** Orbis Books, Maryknoll, New York, 1977.

Discusses the role of the Church in response to the realities of underdevelopment in the Third World. Available on order from your local bookstore or library.

(S)(A) Development and Peace, **International Development and Peace Seminar; Final Report,** Montreal, 1975.

Report on a seminar that focused attention on the problems and causes of underdevelopment in the Third World, the relationship between faith and development, and the role of the Canadian Catholic Organization for Development and Peace. Available on order from Development and Peace, 67 Bond Street, Toronto, Ontario.

(S) Galeano, E., **Open Veins of Latin America,** New York, Monthly Review Press, 1973, 313 pages.

A history of Latin America's experience of colonialism and more recent forms of foreign domination. Available on order from your local bookstore.

(S) Jalée, P., **Le pillage du tiers monde,** Paris, Maspero, 1976, 191 pages.

Une analyse des rapports entre les pays sous-développés et développés. Disponible en librairie.

(S) Lambert, D.C., **Les économies du tiers monde,** Librairie Armand Colin, Paris, 1974.

Un ouvrage sur les théories et les interprétations du sous-développement, et sur les théories visant à expliquer les inégalités de développement. Disponible en bibliothèque.

Latin America

The underdevelopment of Latin America has a history dating back to the sixteenth century when the Spanish and Portuguese empires invaded the Native Indian societies and forced them to become colonies. While the peoples of Latin America did not have the perfect life before colonialism disrupted their societies, the pattern of colonial development left a legacy of problems still evident. To this day, the economies of most Latin American countries are primarily geared to serve the interests of foreign powers rather than the basic needs of life for their populations. The human costs have been poverty, hunger, disease, illiteracy and repression for millions of people. The following resource materials may help to provide some insights on the state of underdevelopment in Latin America.

(S)(A) **Latin America Press,** the English language publication of Noticias Aliadas, APARTADO (P.O. Box) 5594 Lima 1, Peru.

A weekly update of information coming from Latin America. Available by sending subscription to the above address.

(S) **LADOC,** the bimonthly publication of Latin America documentation — United States Catholic Conference. Published by the Office of International Justice and Peace, United States Catholic Conference, 1312 Massachusetts Avenue, N.W., Washington, D.C., 20005.

Provides current information and analysis of Latin American problems, with particular attention to the work of the Church. Available by sending subscription to the above address.

(S)   Gunder Frank, A., **Capitalism and Underdevelopment in Latin America; Historical Studies of Chile and Brazil,** Monthly Review Press, New York, 1969, 344 pages.

A classic on the underdevelopment of Latin America. Available on order from your local bookstore or library.

(A)   **LAWG Letter,** Latin American Working Group, Toronto.

A monthly publication outlining current issues in different Latin American countries. Subscription address: LAWG, Box 2207, Station P, Toronto, M5R 2T2.

(S)   Niedergang, M., **The Twenty Latin Americas (2 vol.),** London, Penguin, 1971, 802 pages.

A collection of dossiers of each Latin American country. Available on order from your local bookstore or library.

(S)   Stavenhagen, R., **Sept thèses erronées sur l'Amérique latine,** Anthropos, Paris, 1973, 205 pages.

Un exposé de différentes analyses des problèmes de développement de l'Amérique latine. Disponible en librairie.

Africa

The roots of underdevelopment in African countries today go back to the European slave trade between the seventeenth and the nineteenth centuries which decimated much of the population of African society. While most African countries have now gained political independence, the scars and structures of European colonialism are still evident. The economies of most African countries are still dominated by foreign powers and apartheid continues to rule in southern Africa. The following resource materials may help to provide some insights into the state of underdevelopment in Africa.

(S)   Arrighi, G. and Saul, J.S., **Essays on the Political Economy of Africa,** Monthly Review Press, New York-London, 1973.

A collection of essays on the political and economic developments in sub-Saharan Africa. Available on order from your local bookstore or library.

(S)   Cartey, W. and Kilson, M., **The Africa Reader: Independent Africa,** Vintage, New York, 1970. 428 pages.

A collection of essays, mostly by Africans, dealing with various independence movements in Africa. Available on order from your local bookstore or library.

(S)   Fanon, F., **Wretched of the Earth,** Grove Publication, New York, 1968, 316 pages.

An in-depth analysis of the social and cultural oppression of the African people. Available on order from your local bookstore.

(S)   Lamont, D., **Speech from the Dock,** Kevin Maythew Ltd., London, 1977, 143 pages.

A statement on the state of racism in southern Africa today by a bishop who openly defied the Rhodesian regime. Available on order from your local bookstore.

(S)   **L'Afrique économique,** INADES (Institut africain pour le développement économique et social), 1978.

Un ouvrage encyclopédique qui se divise en trois parties: une présentation des 54 pays ou territoires du continent; un tableau des biens produits; une liste des grandes organisations politiques et économiques de l'Afrique. Disponible en librairie.

Asia

The underdevelopment of Asian countries today also has a history dating back to the colonialism of foreign powers, particularly in the eighteenth and nineteenth centuries. The economy of India, for example, was developed to serve the industrial interests of the British Empire in the nineteenth century. In several Asian countries, valuable food-producing land was taken over for the production of cash crops like cotton, rubber and jute. To this day, the economies of these countries are still based on the export of cash crops, while millions of Asians are suffering from hunger and starvation.

(S)   Branfman, F., (ed.), **Voices from the Plain of Jars: Life Under an Airbore,** New York, Harper and Row, 1972, 160 pages.

A moving account of human suffering in Indochina, particularly the experience of peasants in Laos during the war. Available from Development Education Centre, 121 Avenue Road, Toronto, M5R 2G3.

(S)   Myrdall Gunnar, **Asian Drama, An Inquiry Into The Poverty Of Nations,** New York, Random House, abridged edition by S.S. King, 1974, 464 pages.

An inquiry revealing the poverty of the Asian people. Available on order from your local bookstore.

(S)   **Religion and Development in Asia,** Marga Institute, Columbo, 1974.

Contains some articles of the underdevelopment of Asian countries. Available on order from you local bookstore.

(S)   Selden, Mark, (ed.), **Remaking Asia,** Pantheon, New York, 1974, 381 pages.

A collection of essays exploring the American impact on the development of Japan, India, and South East Asia in general. Available on order from your local bookstore.

2. Global Economy

"Prompted by new systems of production, national boundaries are breaking down and new economic powers are being born, namely, multi-national enterprises. These enterprises pool their resources and are highly diversified; thus they can operate in such a way that they are answerable to no one and largely independent of national politial authorities; and so they are not subject to controls in matters having to do with the common good. By virtue of their broad range of operation, private institutions of this sort can come to be a new and illicit form of economic domination in the social, cultural and even political realm. Excessive concentrations of resources and powers, already condemned by Pius XI on the 40th Anniversary of **Rerum Novarum** *are now assuming new and definite forms.*
(Paul VI, **Octogesima Adveniens,** 1971)

"We wish to emphasize that the principal guilt for economic dependence of our countries rests with powers, inspired by uncontrolled desire for gain, which leads to economic dictatorship and the 'international imperialism of money' condemned by Pope Puis XI in **Quadregesimo Anno** *and by Pope Paul VI in* **Populorum Progressio.**"
(Latin American Bishops, **Medellin Documents,** Peace, No. 9, 1968)

Today, leaders from most poor countries face enormous obstacles, both internal and external, in the development of their peoples. Yet, the global economic system continues to be the basic structural cause of poverty, oppression and underdevelopment in the Third World. While political independence has been attained, economic forms of colonialism still dominate the lives of people in most Third World countries. Industrialized countries continue to accumulate wealth by extracting valuable raw materials and taking advantage of cheap labour conditions for certain types of manufacturing. Several factors may be cited.

Transnational Corporations

Transnational corporations have emerged as the major institutions facilitating the transfer of wealth-bearing resources from the Third World to the industrialized countries. Today, these corporations possess much of the capital and technology required for the development of raw materials in the poor countries. In large measure, the resources and the wealth they generate are taken out of these countries and transferred to the industrialized nations where they are manufactured into finished products for profitable sales on world markets. Through this process, the economies of the poor countries are made to serve the interests of transnational corporations rather than the basic needs of their people for food, clothing, shelter, employment, education and health care.

(S)(A) Espéret, Gérard, **Les sociétés multinationales I et II,** Dossiers Faim et Développement, nos 15A et 16A, Paris, avril et mai 1973.

Deux dossiers sur le rôle et l'importance des sociétés multinationales. Disponible en bibliothèque.

(S) **Multi-National Corporations in World Development,** New York, United Nations, Economic and Social Affairs Department, Preager Publication, 1974, 200 pages.

A study of the general conditions of social and economic development imposed by the multinational corporations. Available on order from your local bookstore.

(S) Muller, R. and Barnett, R., **Global Reach,** New York, Simon and Shuster, 1974, 508 pages.

An important study on the power and impact of multinational corporations today. Available on order from your local bookstore.

(S) Ordonneau, P., **Les multinationales contre les Etats,** Editions Economie et Humanisme, Editions ouvrières, Paris, 1975.

Une analyse des compagnies transnationales et de leur puissance. Disponible en librairie.

(S)   Ward, B. and Dabos, R., **Only One Earth,** London, Penguin Books, 1972.

Includes an analysis of how the industrialized states are plundering the non-renewable resources of the earth. Available on order from your local bookstore or library.

International Trade

The structures of international trade serve to further facilitate the transfer of wealth from the Third World to the industrialized countries. Industrialized countries have repeatedly refused to pay equitable prices for Third World products (e.g. coffee, cocoa, sugar, tea, rice, tin, copper, etc.) while, at the same time, charging Third World countries escalating prices for their own manufactured products (e.g. tractors, railroad equipment, refined aluminium, steel, etc.). Moreover, those Third World countries which are able to manufacture finished products are frequently excluded from markets in the industrialized countries by a system of tariff structures, quotas, and duties. Today, most Third World countries depend upon international markets for the sale of their resources and their purchasing power has steadily worsened. Faced with these obstacles, some developing countries are striving to become less dependent on international trade and more self-reliant.

(A)(E)   Farine, Philippe, **O.N.U., matières premières et développement I et II,** Faim et Développement, dossiers 25A et 27A, avril 1974 et juin-juillet 1974, Paris.

Deux brefs dossiers sur les problèmes posés par "l'échange inégal".
Disponible en bibliothèque.

(A)   **International Trade: A System of Unequal Exchange,** Development and Peace and the Development Education Centre, 1976, 6 pages.

A short descriptive analysis of world trade structures and their impact on Third World countries. Available on order from Development and Peace, 67 Bond Street, Toronto.

(S)   Laurent, Ph., **La concurrence industrielle du tiers monde,** dans Projet no 127, juillet-août 1978, pp. 802-824.

Un article sur la "montée" des économies du tiers monde en "concurrence" avec les économies développées. Disponible en bibliothèque.

Economic Dependency

As a result, most Third World countries still find themselves caught in the trap of economic dependency and exploitation. Much of their wealth-bearing land and raw materials are directly controlled if not owned outright by transnational corporations. Rather than developing their resources to serve the basic needs of their populations, they are compelled to orient their economies for the extraction and export of valuable resources to the industrialized countries. In turn the poor countries become increasingly dependent upon the industrialized nations to provide them with many of the goods and services they require, at world market prices.

(S)   Bénot, Y., **Qu'est-ce que le développement?** Paris, Maspero, 1973, 185 pages.

Une analyse critique du type de développement actuel et de ses implications.
Disponible en librairie.

(A)   **Development and Underdevelopment: Two Sides of the Same Coin,**
Development and Peace and the Development Education Centre, 1976, 5 pages.

A short descriptive analysis of the processes of underdevelopment and economic dependency. Available on order from Development and Peace, 67 Bond Street, Toronto.

(S)   **Le Tiers Monde accuse ...,** dossier spécial de la revue Economie et Humanisme, no 216, mars 1974, pp. 2-37.

Une série d'articles sur diverses manières de penser le développement mondial du point de vue du tiers monde. Disponible en bibliothèque.

(A)   **Trade Union of the Third World,** England, 1979, 30 minutes, colour, 19 mm.

A film presentation which traces the history of colonialism, international trade, and the economic dependence of poor nations related to industrialized countries. Available on order (purchase or rental) from the Development Education Centre, 121 Avenue Road, Toronto, Ontario.

Canadian Connections

While bearing similar marks of economic dependency, Canada participates as an industrialized nation in the global economy that exploits Third World countries. Increasingly, Canadian-based corporations and financial institutions have taken advantage of investment opportunities, particularly in the Carribean and Latin America, to accumulate more wealth. Between 1965 and 1970, Canadian investment in Latin America expanded from 13.6 to 21.2 percent of this country's total investment abroad. Moreover, Canada has closely aligned itself with the United States in many of the global economic decisions affecting Third World countries.

(S)   **Inside Report: Latin America and the Caribbean,** Toronto, Latin American Working Group and the News Synthesis Project.

A monthly publication on Canadian economic and political relations with the Caribbean and Latin America, based on a variety of documented sources. Available on order from the Latin American Working Group, Box 6300, Station "A", Toronto, Ontario, M5W 1P7.

(S)   **Reflections on UNCTAD IV,** Toronto, GATT-Fly Project, 1976, 21 pages.

An analysis of the Canadian government's participation in the Fourth United Nations Conference on Trade and Development. Available on order from the GATT-Fly Project, 11 Madison Avenue, Toronto, Ontario.

3. Self-Reliant Development

"The mere declaration of independence by the new states has not changed the general conditions for Africa's economic development. Independence has however, sometimes led to strained relations with prosperous nations, through fear that financial and technical aid would restrict the liberty and autonomy gained with independence. The African Nations, like every other state in the same situation are conscious of their needs, but they are also justly and proudly aware of their independence."
(Paul VI, **To the Peoples of Africa,** *No. 21, Oct. 29, 1967)*

"Today, the poor and oppressed peoples are demanding an alternative to the present economic order. The nations of the Third World are calling for a new international economic order based on a just distribution of wealth and power. Greater emphasis is being placed on pursuing more self-reliant models of development in which the resources of Third World countries are to be developed and used to meet basic human needs of their populations. Yet, all too often, the legitimate struggles of people to bring about these necessary changes are impeded by the strategies of powerful corporations and governments that befriend them."
(Canadian Bishops **Message on the Tenth Anniversary of Development and Peace and Populorum Progressio,** *1977)*

To free their peoples from the trap of economic dependency, Third World countries have been searching for alternative models of development. In recent years, some of these countries have been struggling to create new models of development based on self-reliance.

Self-Reliance

As an alternative, some Third World countries are turning to models of development designed to be more self-reliant and less dependent on the global economy over which they have no control. In contrast to export-oriented production, energies are being redirected to develop the land and resources of these countries to serve the basic needs of their populations for food, clothing, shelter, education, health care, employment and other basic necessities of life. To do so, it has been necessary to acquire social ownership and control over their own natural resources and the means of production in their society. In attempting these forms of social transformation, however, developing countries have been faced with strong resistance from the industrialized countries.

(S)   Galtang, J., **Implementing Self-Reliance,** in Church Alert, No. 21, October-December 1978.

An analysis of some basic structural problems of self-reliance encountered by Third World countries in the global economic system. Available on order from Church Alert, c/o Sodepax, 150 route de Ferney, 1211 Geneva 20, Switzerland.

(S)   Schumacher, E.F., **Small is Beautiful,** Blond and Briggs, London, 1973.

One of the more recent studies on self-reliant development for societies to serve human needs. Available on order from your local bookstore or library.

(S)(A) **Self-Reliance,** Pontifical Commission for Justice and Peace, Vatican City, 1978.

Prepared for the Third Development Decade of the United Nations this document outlines the Church's teaching on self-reliance in economic development. Available on order from your Catholic bookstore.

(S) Tévoédjrè, A., **La pauvreté, richesse des peuples,** Ed. Economie et Humanisme, Editions ouvrières, Paris, 1978.

Un ouvrage remettant en question le modèle classique de développement qualifié de contre-développement. Disponible en bibliothèque.

(S) Ul Haq, M., **The Poverty Curtain: Choices for the Third World,** New York, Columbia University Press, 1976, 219 pages.

A critique of traditional models of economic development and proposals for self-reliance models of development oriented to serve basic human needs. Available on order from your local bookstore or library.

The Case of Tanzania

In Tanzania, the government of Julius Neyere has launched major social transformations based on the philosophy of self-reliance. Following independence from Britain in 1961, production in this agrarian society was changed from its emphasis on producing cash crops for export to producing food and other basic necessities of life for its own population. Foreign investment and aid were still welcome, provided they complied with the basic needs and priorities of Tanzania's economy. The Tanzanian experiment, however, encountered numerous obstacles in obtaining adequate credit, loans, aid as well as investment from industrialized countries.

(S) **Socialist Planning in Tanzania,** Tanzania Publishing House, Dar Es Salaam, 1972.

A collection of essays on the Tanzanian experience. Available on order from your local bookstore or library.

(S) **The Silent Class Struggle,** Tanzania Publishing House, Dar Es Salaam, 1972.

(E) Urfer, Sylvain, **Une Afrique socialiste: la Tanzanie,** Editions ouvrières, Paris, 1976.

Un essai sur l'expérience socialiste en Tanzanie. Disponible en librairie.

(E) Urfer, Sylvain, **Ujuama espoir du socialisme africain en Tanzanie,** Aubier Montaigne, Paris, 1977.

Un essai sur le mouvement Ujuama sur lequel est basé le modèle tanzanien. Disponible en librairie.

Projects in Self-Reliance

In many Third World countries today, people are striving to overcome problems of dependency and underdevelopment through projects in self-reliant development. Through various co-operatives projects and other forms of communal ownership and control, peasants and workers are exercising self-determination in rural and urban communities of some countries. In a few cases, major land reforms have provided opportunities for peasants to develop farming, fishing, and cattle breeding industries. In other cases, people have organized education, health care, and housing projects designed to serve the real needs of their communities. And there are also some examples of workers who have organized to develop and control small factories and industries.*

(S)(A) **Betting on the Weak,** Commission on the Churches' Participation in Development, Switzerland, 1976.

A collection of short case studies on projects in self-reliant development in several Third World countries. Available on order from the World Council of Churches Commission on the Churches' Participation in Development, 150 route de Ferney, 1121 Geneva 20, Switzerland.

(A)   **Education in Self-Reliance,** Development and Peace and the Development Education Centre, Toronto, 1976, 6 pages.

A resumé of the kind of education in self-reliance taking place in some Third World countries. Available on order from Development and Peace, 67 Bond Street, Toronto, Ontario.

*Note: A large portion of funds collected by the Canadian Catholic Organization for Development and Peace is contributed to socio-economic projects based on self-reliance in Third World countries. Development and Peace has contributed to self-reliance projects in community development, agriculture, cattle breeding and fisheries, co-operative movements, health and welfare, literacy and education and a variety of small industries. For further information, contact Développement et Paix, 2111 rue Centre, Montréal, Québec, H3K 1J5 (Tel.: 514-932-5136).

New World Order?

In the United Nations, the developing countries of the Third World have proposed some basic reforms in the international economic and political order. The U.N. Declaration for a New International Economic Order calls for self-determination and the right of developing countries to (a) control their resources and the wealth they generate and (b) re-orient their economies to serve the development needs of their people and assert their sovereignty over the operations of transnational corporations in their countries. In effect, the U.N. Declaration provides a general framework of reforms which could assist the poor nations in advancing their strategies for self-reliant development. For the most part, however, the industrialized countries and transnational corporations have either ignored, delayed, or resisted any significant changes required in the present global economy.

(S)(A) Cosmao, V., **Dossier "Nouvel ordre mondial": les chrétiens provoqués par le développement,** Ed. Chalet, Lyon, 1978.

Un recueil d'articles sur l'organisation économique du monde actuel et les possibilités d'un nouvel ordre économique. Disponible en bibliothèque.

(A)   **Le nouvel ordre économique international,** diaporama (80 dia., 15 min., cassette), Développement et Paix, Montréal.

Un instrument de travail pour une réflexion sur ce thème. Disponible à Développement et Paix, 2111 rue Centre, Montréal, H3K 1J5.

(S)   Gremillion, J. and Ryan, W., (Eds.) **World Faiths and the New World Order,** Interreligions Peace Colloquium, Lisbon, 1978, 248 pages.

A collection of papers on the demands for a new world order to serve basic human needs and the corresponding challenges to the major religious faiths. Available on order from your local bookstore or library.

(A)   **What is the New International Economic Order?,** GATT-Fly Project, 1975, 20 pages.

An overview of the history and the proposals for a "new international economic order". Available on order from the GATT-Fly Project, 11 Madison Avenue, Toronto, Ontario.

(A)   Sodepax, **In Search of a New Society: Christian Participation in the Building of New Relationships among Peoples,** in Church Alert, No. 8, May 1976.

A document pertaining to the need for new world order, prepared jointly by the Pontifical Justice and Peace Commission and the Justice and Service Committee of the World Council of Churches. Available on order from SODEPAX, Ecumenical Center, P.O.B. 86, 150 route de Ferney, 1211 Genève, Suisse. Other editions of Church Alert focus on the question of a new international economic order. See, for example, No. 16.

4. Foreign Aid

"... and the receiving countries could demand that there be no interference in their political life or subversion of their social structures. As sovereign states, they have a right to conduct their own affairs...."
(Paul VI, **Populorum Progressio,** No. 54, 1967)

In recent years, there have been significant increases in the amount of aid flowing from the rich nations to the poor. In the same years however, the gap has continued to grow between the developed and the underdeveloped countries. Foreign aid, in its present form, fails to confront problems of illiteracy, malnutrition, social inequalities, disease and unemployment. Instead, it has become an instrument for the underdevelopment of many Third World countries, making them more and more economically dependent on the industrialized nations. Several factors may be cited.

Business Aid

For most industrialized countries, foreign aid is not an act of charity. It is an instrument to promote the business and commercial interests of their own countries in the Third World. For most foreign aid is really "tied aid", tied to the purchase of goods and services made in the industrialized countries. In receiving this type of "aid", poor countries are compelled to spend most of the money to purchase products from the donor country (which may not be the cheapest, nor the most suitable products available) and to purchase the costly services of technical personnel (e.g. consultants, engineers, architects, etc.) from the donor country. In effect, foreign aid has become a business enterprise for the industrialized countries, designed to stimulate overseas markets for their own industries. Some maintain that multi-lateral aid, which is mediated through international agencies, provides greater flexibility and less economic and political constraints than bilateral aid programmes between individual nations. However, the major multilateral agencies such as the World Bank, the International Monetary Fund, and the Inter-American Development Bank are all controlled by the donors, namely, the industrial countries themselves. As a result, multilateral aid is generally tied to economic constraints.

(A)   **Aid: The New Trojan Horse,** Development and Peace and Development Education Centre, 1976, 5 pages.

A short descriptive analysis of how foreign aid programmes affect Third World countries. Available on order from Development and Peace, 67 Bond Street, Toronto.

(S)   Goulet, D. and Hudson, M., **The Myth of Aid: the Hidden Agenda of Development Reports,** prepared by the Center for Study of Development and Social Change, IDOC North America, New York, 1971, 143 pages.

A critical look at foreign aid. Available on order from your local library.

(A)   **How Much Help is Foreign Aid?** Clyde Sanger, Ten Days for World Development, 1977, 5 pages.

Available on order from Ten Days for World Development, 600 Jarvis Street, Toronto.

Canadian Aid

Canadian aid has generally followed the same pattern. In recent years, between 80 and 90 percent of Canada's bilateral aid programme, which channels most of the Canadian government's overseas aid to Third World countries has been tied to purchases in Canada. It is estimated that approximately two thirds of Canadian bilateral aid to the Third World is spent right here in Canada on goods, commodities, and services. Most of Canada's "aid", therefore, never really leaves this country but is funneled directly into Canadian business. Moreover, the Canadian government's Export Development

Corporation, which lends money to foreign buyers, makes loans that are also tied to the purchase of Canadian goods and services. And, while it may appear that the EDC is helping to finance Third World companies which need capital, a closer look sometimes reveals that those companies receiving the loans are subsidiaries of Canadian or American transnational corporations. In effect, Canada's aid and loan programmes affecting Third World countries, help to further facilitate the accumulation of wealth for Canadian businesses and perpetuate patterns of economic dependency for Third World countries.

(S) **Canada Strategy for International Development Cooperation 1975-1980,** C.I.D.A., Information Canada, Ottawa, 1975, 48 pages.

This document outlines the Canadian government's basic aid programme and strategy. Available from C.I.D.A., Place du Centre, 200 rue Principale, Hull.

(S) **Canadian Aid: Blessing or Burden,** Toronto, LAWG Letter, Vol. III, No. 4, April 1976, pages 3-10.

An analysis of the interests behind Canadian aid and the expansion of Canadian corporations in the Third World. Available from LAWG, Box 2207, Station "P", Toronto, M5S 2T2.

(E) Midy, F., **L'aide du Canada au développement international,** SUCO, Montréal, 1973.

Historique, objectif, évolution et orientation politique. Disponible en consultation au secrétariat national de Développement et Paix, 2111 rue Centre, Montréal.

(S) **North-South Encounter: the Third World and Canadian Performance,** in Canada North-South 1977-1978, the North-South Institute, Ottawa, 1977, 200 pages.

An analysis of Canada's relations with developing countries. Available at your local bookstore.

(E) Palacios, A. et Martinez, L., **L'aide canadienne; quelles en sont les priorités?** Québec, 1973.

Une étude des relations entre les organisations non gouvernementales, les intérêts économiques et leurs implications pour l'Amérique latine. Disponible en consultation au secrétariat national de Développement et Paix, 2111 rue Centre, Montréal.

(S) Sabourin, L., **Analyse des politiques de coopération internationale du Canada,** dans **Le Canada et le Québec sur la scène internationale,** Painchaud, P. (dir.), Montréal, Presses de l'Université du Québec, 1977, pages 209-222.

Une analyse critique de la stratégie d'aide du gouvernement canadien. Disponible en librairie.

Some Christian Education-Action Programmes

Development and Peace has been the Church's major programme for education and action on the question of aid to Third World countries. Development and Peace's projects for socio-economic development provide a viable alternative to government foreign aid programmes by funds to specific socio-economic projects in communities, without economic conditions attached. This form of aid is designed to go directly to the people in need. Moreover, most of the socio-economic projects funded by Development and Peace are community projects in self-reliant development. Development and Peace also sponsors a year-round education and awareness programme on the problems of underdevelopment in the Third World, including the issue of foreign aid. Development and Peace committees are active in almost every region of Canada and full-time animators serve as resource persons for the education-action programmes of these committees. In most regions, local Development and Peace committees are engaged in both the socio-economic projects and the education programmes of Development and Peace.

*For further information, contact: Development and Peace, 67 Bond Street, Toronto, Ontario, (Tel.: 416-868-0540) and Jeunes du Monde, C.P. 220, Limoilou, Québec, G1L 4V7 (Tel.: 418-529-4924).

Some Questions for Animators:

1. What are some of the basic problems experienced by specific Third World peoples concerning the foreign aid programmes of industrialized countries? Have you or your group had some practical experience in educating and acting on these issues?

2. What research or studies are most useful for analyzing the inadequacies of present foreign aid programmes? Canada's foreign aid programmes? What are the conclusions of these studies?

3. What critical insights can be found in the Scriptures or the social teachings of the Church? What particular ethical or theological judgments can be made?

4. What can be done to develop more critical awareness among Christians in your community or region on the issue of foreign aid? What types of programmes can be developed for education and action on these issues? What kind of resources or tools for animation are most helpful?

5. What kind of organizations are directly involved in education and action on the issues of foreign aid? What kinds of co-operation or working relationships can be developed with these groups?

6. What relevant connections can be made between the injustices of foreign aid and similar problems faced by the poor in our own society? or region?

7. What forms of action might be taken by Christian groups in your community to change the policies of the Canadian government on issues like "tied-aid"?

5. International Trade

"One must avoid the risk of increasing still more the wealth of the rich and the dominion of the strong, whilst leaving the poor in their misery and adding to the servitude of the oppressed.

...nations whose industrialization is limited are faced with serious difficulties when they have to rely on their exports to balance their economy and to carry out their plans for development. The poor nations remain ever poor while the rich ones become still richer."
(Paul VI, **Populorum Progressio,** No. 33, 57, 1967)

Over the past two decades at the United Nations Conference on Trade and Development, the poor countries of the Third World have put forward proposals demanding fundamental changes in the inequitable structures of world trade. The response of the rich industrialized countries, for the most part, has been to resist basic change and to stabilize the patterns of inequality and dependency in the structures of international trade.

Maintaining Inequality and Dependency

The industrialized countries have often blocked the efforts of Third World countries to improve their terms of trade. After numerous commodity negotiations and agreements (e.g. for cocoa, sugar, coffee and tea, etc.) the prices which the producing Third World countries receive for their products remain proportionately far less than the prices they have to pay for rapidly rising costs of importing manufactured goods. Proposals to index the prices of Third World commodities, by tying them to the increases in the costs of manufactured products, have been resisted by most of the major industrialized countries. Efforts on the part of the producers of coffee, cocoa, tea and bauxite to follow the OPEC example of forming producer associations to improve their export earnings, have been met with threats of retaliation on the part of several industrialized nations. Moreover, the attempts of some Third World countries to further process their primary products before exporting them, have been thwarted by industrialized countries imposing tariff structures such as import duties which severely limit the possibilities of selling these products. And these injustices are multiplied by the fact that developing countries, whose economies have been oriented for exports, are almost totally dependent on world trade structures for their very survival.

(S) **Commodity Trade: Test Case for an New Economic Order,** in Canada North-South, 1977-1978, North-South Institute, Ottawa, 1978, 100 pages.

This report analyses the workings of the commodity trade system and establishes Canada's vital stake in world competition and co-operation. Available on order from your local bookstore or library.

(A) **Commodity Profile,** Toronto, GATT-Fly Project, 1976.

An analysis of the political and economic forces determining coffee prices and the consequences for agricultural workers in producing countries. Available on order from the GATT-Fly Project, 11 Madison Avenue, Toronto, Ontario.

(A) **International Trade: A System of Unequal Exchange,** Development and Peace and the Development Education Centre, Toronto, 1976, 6 pages.

A short descriptive analysis of world trade structures and their impact on Third World countries.

(S) **Les dominations économiques et l'auto-développement,** dossier spécial dans Economie et Humanisme, no 205, mai-juin 1972, pp. 2-45.

Une série d'articles sur divers aspects du développement actuel. Disponible en bibliothèque.

(S) **Problèmes du développement,** dossier spécial dans Economie et Humanisme, no 225, septembre-octobre 1975, pp. 2-41.

Un dossier sur les problèmes de développement des pays du tiers monde. Disponible en bibliothèque.

(S)(A) **Sugar and Sugarworkers,** GATT-Fly Project, 1978.

A three-part kit on: How the International Sugar Economy Works; Sugarworkers Around the World; The Future of Sugar. Available on order from the GATT-Fly Project, 11 Madison Avenue, Toronto, Ontario.

Canadian Trade Practices

Although Canada shares some similarities with Third World countries as a primary exporter of raw materials, Canada has consistently joined with other industrialized countries in resisting basic changes in trade structures. In the United Nations Conferences on Trade and Development, for example, Canada has rejected the principle that every country has the sovereign right to freely trade with other countries and to freely dispose of its natural resources in the interests of the economic development and well-being of its own people. In commodity negotiations, Canada has often taken a hard-line position, notably in negotiations on price increases for Third World sugar. While the Canadian government has expressed some concern for indexing commodity prices, it has so far refused to support the proposals put forward by the Third World countries. And Canadian tariffs, such as quotas on textiles and clothing from Asian countries, have placed limits on the marketing of Third World products here in Canada.

(S) **A Brief to the Canadian Trade and Tariffs Committee,** Toronto, GATT-Fly Project, 1975, 13 pages.

A set of proposed changes in Canadian tariff policies for the benefit of both Canada and Third World countries. Available from GATT-Fly Project, 11 Madison Avenue, Toronto, Ontario, M5R 2S2.

(S) **Canada vs tiers monde: des relations marginales?** Centre d'étude et de coopération internationale, mars-avril 1978, dossiers nos 26-27.

Un examen global sur les relations du Canada avec les pays du tiers monde. Disponible au Centre d'étude et de coopération internationale, 4824 chemin Côte-des-Neiges, Montréal, Québec, H3V 1G4.

(A) Clarke, A. and others, **Canada and The Trade Issue,** Ottawa, Canadian Council for International Co-operation, 1974, 54 pages.

A useful introduction to Canadian trade policies and their impact on Third World countries. Available from the Canadian Council for International Co-operation, 321 Chapel Street, Ottawa, Ontario, K1N 2Z2.

(S) **Reflections on UNCTAD IV,** Toronto, GATT-Fly Project, 1976, 21 pages.

A critical analysis of global trade negotiations and Canada's role in them. Available from GATT-Fly Project, 11 Madison Avenue, Toronto, M5R 2S2.

Some Christian Education-Action Programmes

Following the Third United Nations Conference on Trade and Development in 1972, the Churches became involved in raising critical ethical questions about the injustices of international trade. Under the sponsorship of the major Churches the GATT-Fly Project conducted research on how trade structures perpetuate the economic dependency of Third World countries. Specific research papers were prepared on Third World commodities (e.g. sugar, cocoa, coffee), Canadian trade and tariff policies, and a variety of related issues. Along with other groups, the GATT-Fly Project also played a major role at such events as — the World Food Conference (1974), the Seventh Special Session of the United Nations on a New Economic Order (1975), and the Fourth United Nations Conference on Trade and Development (1976) — pressing the Canadian government to respond to the demands of the Third World countries. More recently, le Centre d'étude et de coopération internationale in Quebec has prepared various background papers on international trade issues which have been used by Christian groups for study and animation.

*For more information, contact: GATT-Fly Project, 11 Madison Avenue, Toronto, Ontario, M5R 2S2 (Tel.: 416-921-4615); Development and Peace, education co-ordinator, 67 Bond Street, Toronto, Ontario (Tel.: 416-868-0540); Le Centre d'étude et de coopération internationale, 4824 chemin Côte-des-Neiges, Montréal, Québec, H3V 1G4. The GATT-Fly Project also publishes a monthly newsletter **Flying Together** (available on order from the above address).

Some Questions for Animators:

1. What are some of the injustices suffered by Third World peoples in dealing with the structures of international trade? Have you or your group had any practical experience in educating and acting on these issues?

2. What research or studies are useful for analyzing the injustices of international trade? Canada's trade policies? What are the conclusions of these studies?

3. What critical insights can be found in the Scriptures or the social teachings of the Church? What specific ethical or theological judgments can be made about global trade structures?

4. What can be done to develop a more critical awareness among people in your community or region on these issues of international trade? What types of programmes can be developed for education and action?

5. What kind of organizations are directly involved in education and action on the issues of world trade and economic justice? What kinds of co-operation or working relationships can be developed with these groups?

6. What relevant connections can be made between the injustices of international trade and similar injustices encountered by poor people or poor regions in our own country?

7. What forms of action might be taken to change the policies and position of the Canadian government on specific trade issues that perpetuate underdevelopment and dependency of Third World countries?

6. Foreign Investment

"Some foreign companies working in our country (also some national firms) often evade the established tax system by subterfuge. We are also aware that at times they send their profits and dividends abroad, without contributing adequate reinvestments to the progressive development of our countries.
(Latin American Bishops, **Medellin Documents,** *Peace, No. 8c, 1968)*

"In both Canada and the Third World, powerful corporations are planning the use of natural resources without the participation of the people who are most directly affected ... The consequences of the present order are dependency, loss of human dignity, poverty and even starvation."
(Canadian Church Leaders, **Justice Demands Action,** *1976)*

The investment of transnational corporations in many Third World countries have often proven to be more of an obstacle to the real development of people. While the transnationals possess the capital and technology required for industrialization, their basic priorities are the accumulation of more wealth. Through foreign investment, the economies of many Third World countries have been directed to serve the interests of transnational corporations rather than the development needs of their populations.

Social and Economic Costs

Studies show that the investment of transnational corporations has had a variety of negative impacts on the social and economic life of many Third World countries. Several examples can be briefly cited: the further directing of local economic priorities towards export rather than self-reliant development; the creation of jobs that divert the productive capacities of people away from serving local needs; the priorities of some key industries to produce luxury goods and promote luxury consumption; the extraction and export of wealth-bearing raw materials rather than manufacturing them within the poor countries themselves; the exploitation of cheap labour conditions by creating low-paying jobs rather than paying wages required in the industrialized countries; the demands for generous investment incentives from local governments (e.g. tax holidays, provision of infrastructures such as railroads, electrical systems, communication networks, port facilities) that further divert public funds away from providing the kinds of social services desparately needed by millions of people; the drainage of profits made on operations in poor countries for investments elsewhere rather than contributing capital required for local development needs. While the social and economic costs vary from place to place, the general pattern and their effects tend to be similar in most Third World countries.

(S) Bertin, G.Y., **L'investissement international,** Presses universitaires de France, coll. Que sais-je, no 1256, Paris, 1967, 128 pages.

Un bref exposé sur les différents types d'investissements étrangers. Disponible en bibliothèque.

(A)   **Controlling Interest: The World of the Multinational Corporation.**

A film that dramatically describes the power and the social impact of the transnational corporation. Distributed in Canada by the United Church of Canada, 85 St Clair Avenue East, Toronto, Ontario.

(A)   **Foreign Investment: For What? For Whom?** Development and Peace and the Development Education Centre, Toronto, 1976, page 6.

A useful guide for analyzing the economic, social, and political impact of foreign investment in the Third World with references to the operations of Canadian companies. Available from Development and Peace, 67 Bond Street, Toronto.

(S)   **Multi-National Corporations in World Development,** New York, United Nations, Economic and Social Affairs Department, Preager Publications, 1974, 200 pages.

A study of the general conditions of social and economic development imposed by the multinational corporations. Available on order from your local bookstore.

*See also **Global Reach** in Global Economy, section above.

Canadian Investment

Increasingly, Canadian-based corporations have been extending their operations to Third World countries, principally in Latin America where close to 90 percent of Canadian in the Third World is concentrated. Canadian mining companies have made substantial investments in several Latin American countries and secured control over strategic supplies of raw materials for future extraction and export. For many years, a Canadian-owned corporation was one of the largest transnationals operating in Brazil and had a major impact on the development of a dependent economy in that country. Moreover, Canadian manufacturing industries exploit cheap labour conditions in countries like Taiwan and SriLanka, paying low wages and retaining higher profits. In these and other ways, Canadian-based corporations accumulate more wealth through investments in Third World countries and thereby tend to help further the retarded development and economic dependency of those countries.

(A)   **L'Alcan: une multinationale comme les autres,** 80 dia., 15 min., bobine, produit par Développement et Paix.

Le comportement oppressif d'une multinationale. Disponible à Développement et Paix, 2111 rue Centre, Montréal, Québec, H3K 1J5.

(S)   Deverell, J., **Falconbridge: Portrait of a Canadian Mining Multinational,** Toronto, Lorimer Company Press, 1976.

A case study of Falconbridge Company and the social and economic impact of its operations in the Dominican Republic and Namibia. Available on order from your local bookstore.

(S)   Swift, J. and Development Education Centre, **The Big Nickel: Inco at Home and Abroad,** Toronto, Between the Lines, 1978.

A case study of Inco including its operation in Guatemala and Indonesia. Available from Development Education Centre, 121 Avenue Road, Toronto, Ontario, M5R 2G3.

(S)   **The Dark Side of the Light,** LAWG Letter, Vol. IV, No. 2, December 1976.

An analysis of the former operations of the Brascan Company in Brazil. Available on order from LAWG, Box 2207, Station "P", Toronto, Ontario, M5S 2T2.

(S)(A) **We Stand on Guard...from Whom?** Toronto, GATT-Fly Project, 1976.

A collection of seven articles which examines the involvement of Canadian corporations in the control of resource development in both the Amazon region of Brazil and the Northwest Territories. Available on order from GATT-Fly Project, 11 Madison Avenue, Toronto, Ontario.

(S) **Worlds Apart, Human Rights and Economic Relations: Canada-Chile,** LAWG
Letter, Vol. V, Nos. 4-5, May-June 1978.

A study demonstrating the shocking growth of Canadian business and
governmental support for the Chilean dictatorship. Available from LAWG,
Box 2207, Station "P", Toronto, Ontario, M5S 2T2.

Some Christian Education-Action Programmes

The Church has been actively engaged in raising ethical questions about the
operations of Canadian-based corporations in specific Third World countries.
The Task Force on Churches and Corporate Responsibility has been assisting
Christian groups, who are shareholders in various Canadian corporations, to
raise questions and press for changes in the unjust practices of such
corporations in Third World countries. Case studies have been prepared on the
operations of specific corporations, in meetings have been held between
Church representatives and the management of various corporations, and
presentations have been made to the annual shareholders' meetings of the
companies in question. More recently local Church groups in several parts of
the country have actively participated in the work of the Task Force, thereby
increasing public awareness about the operations of Canadian-based
corporations in the Third World. In addition, the GATT-Fly Project has done
research on the social and economic costs of major resource development
projects in countries like Brazil, Peru and Mexico.

*For more information, contact: Task Force on Churches and Corporate
Responsibility, c/o 600 Jarvis Street, Toronto, Ontario, M4Y 2J6
(Tel.: 416-923-1758); Development and Peace, Education Co-ordinator,
67 Bond Street, Toronto, Ontario (Tel.: 416-868-0540). The Task Force on
Churches and Corporate Responsibility also publishes a monthly newsletter
Ticker Tape (available on order from the above address).

Some Questions for Animators:

1. What are some of the problems of underdevelopment caused by the operations
    of transnational corporations in specific Third World countries? Have you or
    your group had any practical experience in educating and acting on these
    issues?

2. What research or studies are useful for analyzing transnational corporations
    and the problems of underdevelopment in Third World countries? Canadian
    transnational corporations? What are the conclusions of these studies?

3. What critical insights can be found in the Scriptures or the social teachings of
    the Church? What specific ethical or theological judgments can be made on
    these issues?

4. What can be done to develop more critical awareness among Christians in
    your community or region on the issues of foreign investment in Third World
    countries? What types of programmes can be initiated for education and
    action on this issue?

5. What kind of organizations are directly involved in education and action on the
    unjust operations of transnational corporations in Third World countries. What
    kinds of co-operation or working relationship can be developed with these
    groups?

6. What relevant connections can be made between the injustices of foreign
    investment in Third World countries and the operations of some foreign-owned
    corporations here in Canada or your own region?

7. What forms of action might be taken by Christian groups in your community
    to change the policies and practices of Canadian-based corporations operating
    in Third World countries?

7. World Hunger

"Today no one can be ignorant any longer of the fact that in whole continents countless men and women are ravished by hunger, countless numbers of children are undernourished, so that many of them die in infancy, while the physical growth and mental development of many others are retarded and as a result whole regions are condemned to the most depressing despondency."
(Paul VI, **Populorum Progressio,** No. 45, 1967)

"The world food crisis will not be solved without the participation of the agricultural workers, and this cannot be complete and fruitful without a radical revision of the underestimation by the modern world of the importance of agriculture."
(Paul VI, **Address to the World Food Conference,** Rome, 1974)

"We known we cannot in conscience stand idly by while fellow human beings die from hunger. That would be a cruel denial to our neighbors of the most fundamental of all needs — the need to eat in order to live"
(Canadian Bishops, **Sharing Daily Bread,** 1974)

The realities of hunger and starvation throughout the Third World today are a symptom of the structures of underdevelopment and dependence experienced by the poor countries. While many "causes" of world hunger have been cited — expanding population, poor climatic conditions, inadequate food-producing technologies, wasteful consumption, inequitable distribution of land — the basic causes lie in the political and economic structures that perpetuate underdevelopment.

Food Dependence

Today, it is estimated that most Third World countries could produce enough food to feed their people if they were not trapped in colonial agricultural patterns. In most of the poor countries, the best land is taken up for the production of cash crops and the relatively poor agricultural land is left over for the production of food for local needs. The food-producing land itself is primarily owned and controlled by small wealthy elites. Indeed, there are an estimated 100 million landless rural dwellers in the Third World and a very small number of land-holding peasants able to fully feed themselves and their families on what they produce. Instead of utilizing good agricultural land to produce food for domestic needs, Third World countries have become increasingly dependent on food imports from the industrialized countries. In most of the poor countries therefore, radical land reforms, in which ownership and control of agricultural land and production are placed in the hands of the agricultural workers, are a necessary step to reverse the cause of hunger and starvation.

(S)   Dumont, R., **La croissance de la famine,** Seuil, Paris, 1975, 191 pages.

Un livre sur la famine et sur certains éléments de solution à ce problème. Disponible en librairie.

(S)   George, Susan, **How the Other Half Dies,** Penguin Books, London, 1976, 349 pages.

A major study on the economic and political mechanism of world hunger. Available on order from your local bookstore.

(S)(A)   **L'agro-business en Amérique latine: l'industrialisation de la terre,** dossier spécial comprenant des articles de Gonzolo Arroyo et alii, dans le **Monde Diplomatique,** septembre 1978, pp. 5-9.

Une série d'articles sur l'expansion de l'agro-business en Amérique latine au détriment des besoins locaux. Disponible en bibliothèque.

(A)   **L'arme du blé,** film 16 mm, 57 min., réalisé par la télévision française (3e chaîne), 1976.

Un film montrant le contrôle réel de 6 firmes multinationales sur le marché mondial du blé. Disponible à Développement et Paix, 2111 rue Centre, Montréal, Québec, H3K 1J5.

(A)   **Land, People and Power: The Question of Third World Land Reform,** Oxfam Publication, 1977.

Provides three case studies of land reform: Guatemala, India, China. Available on order from Oxfam-Ontario, 175 Carlton Street, Toronto, Ontario, M5A 2K3.

(S)(A) Lappé, F. and Collins, J., **Food First,** Houghton Mifflin, Boston. 1976.

An important study on food and agricultural policies in relation to problems of world hunger. Available on order from your local bookstore or library.

(A)   **When did we see you hungry?** Ten Days for World Development/1978 Leaders' Kit, Toronto, Inter-Church Committee for World Development Education, 1978.

Contains a series of highly readable and informative articles on the causes of world hunger and the theological reasons for actively opposing them. Available from Inter-Church Committee for World Development Education, 600 Jarvis Street, Room 219, Toronto, Ontario, M4Y 2J8.

Canadian Food Policies

Responding to the problems of world hunger, the Canadian government has substantially increased its food aid and agricultural assistance programmes. Yet, these initiatives tend to perpetuate the patterns and structures of food dependency. While providing food aid for emergency relief is certainly important in itself, it must also be recognized that Canada's food aid policies, like those of most other industrialized countries', are largely designed to promote commercial markets for Canadian agricultural products. While up to 33 percent of Canada's bilateral funds will go into agricultural assistance over the next five years, the problems of food dependency will be furthered since 80 percent of Canada's bilateral funding is "tied" to the purchase of Canadian products and technical advisors which may not be the most effective means for increasing food production in certain poor countries. In announcing these initiatives at the 1974 World Food Conference, the Canadian government joined with other industrialized countries in strongly resisting demands for basic structural changes in the world market system, which will be necessary if the hungry nations are going to break the yoke of food dependency.

(S)(A) **Canada's Food Trade — By Bread Alone?** GATT-Fly Project, August 1978, Toronto, 4 pages.

An analysis of the general Canadian agricultural and food trade pattern. Available on order from GATT-Fly Project, 11 Madison Avenue, Toronto, M5R 2S2.

(S)   Government of Canada, Agriculture Canada, Consumer and Corporate Affairs Canada, **A Food Strategy for Canada,** Supply and Services Canada, Ottawa, Ontario, 1977, 21 pages.

An exposé of the Canadian strategy. Available on order from your local bookstore or the Government of Canada.

(A)   **How Sweet it is! Ti-Redpath va à la Côte d'Ivoire,** GATT-Flyer, no 4.

Un examen critique du rôle d'une entreprise canadienne dans l'implantation et le développement de l'industrie sucrière en Côte d'Ivoire et en Afrique de l'Ouest. Disponible à GATT-Fly Project, 11 Madison Avenue, Toronto, Ontario, M5R 2S2.

(S)   **Reflections on the World Food Conference,** GATT-Fly Project, 1975, 25 pages.

A critical analysis of the role of Canada and the industrialized countries at the 1974 World Food Conference. Available on order from the GATT-Fly Project, 11 Madison Avenue, Toronto, Ontario, M5R 2S2.

(S)   **World Food and the Canadian "Breadbasket",** in the North-South 1977-1978, the North-South Institute, Ottawa, Ontario, 1978, 68 pages.

A study of global food problems and Canada's role as a food-producing nation. Available on order from your local bookstore or library.

Some Christian Education-Action Programmes

Following the 1974 World Food Conference, the Churches launched a major public awareness programme on the problems and causes of world hunger. Development and Peace, choosing food as the central theme of its programme, prepared animation tools and education projects. Ten Days for World Development, an ecumenical education project of the Churches' development and relief agencies, became a major vehicle for education and action. For the past two years, Ten Days' committees active in various community centers and regions of the country, organized numerous public education events during Lent. In Quebec, Développement et Paix organized similar public awareness events highlighting the issues of world hunger. Events included speakers from Third World countries, seminars and conferences on the causes of hunger, and study-action projects on local problems of food production and marketing. Moreover, the GATT-Fly Project has done some extensive research on Canada's agricultural trade policies and their impact on Third World countries.

*For further information, contact: Ten Days for World Development, c/o 600 Jarvis Street, Toronto, Ontario, M4Y 2J6 (Tel.: 416-922-0591); Development and Peace, Education Co-ordinator, 67 Bond Street, Toronto, Ontario (Tel.: 416-868-0540); GATT-Fly Project, 11 Madison Avenue, Toronto, Ontario, M5R 2S3 (Tel.: 416-921-4615).

Some Questions for Animators:

1. What are some specific examples of Third World peoples suffering from the problems of hunger, malnutrition and starvation? Have you or your group had some practical experience in educating and acting on these problems?

2. What research or studies are helpful for analyzing the causes of hunger and the problems of food production in Third World countries? Canada's food policies? What are the conclusions of these studies?

3. What critical insights can be found in the Scriptures or the social teachings of the Church? What specific ethical or theological judgments can be made about the problems and causes of hunger?

4. What can be done to develop more critical awareness among Christians in your community or region on the issues of world hunger? What types of programmes can be developed for education and action on these issues? What methods and tools for animation are most helpful?

5. What kinds of organizations are directly engaged in education and action on the problems and causes of world hunger? What kinds of co-operation or working relationship can be developed with these groups?

6. What relevant connections can be made between the problems of food production in Third World countries and the problems faced by small farmers and fishermen engaged in food production in our own society or region?

7. What forms of action might be taken by Christian groups in your community to change the policies of the Canadian government concerning agricultural assistance to Third World countries or the operations of Canadian agribusiness corporations?

8. Repression of Human Rights

"Justice is also being violated by forms of oppression, both old and new, springing from restriction of the rights of individuals. This is occurring both in the form of repression by the political power and of violence on the part of private reaction, and can reach the extreme of affecting the basic conditions of personal integrity. There are well-known cases of torture, especially of political prisoners, who besides are frequently denied due process or who are subjected to arbitrary procedures in their trial. Nor can we pass over the prisoners of war who even after the Geneva Convention are being treated in an inhuman manner."
(Justice in the World, No. 24, 1971)

"...The continued oppression of black people under the apartheid regime of South Africa and the repression of people under the military Junta of Chile are but two examples of the pastoral problems which we are addressing in the Third World today. In these and related situations, we believe that the Churches in Canada have a pastoral responsibility to raise ethical questions about the operations of the Canadian government and Canadian-based corporations in these countries. Our primary concern is to see that these Canadian institutions do not serve to strengthen the structures of oppression and the underdevelopment of peoples within those countries."
(Letter of the Canadian Conference of Catholic Bishops to the Bank of Montreal, *1978)*

The widespread repression of human rights evident in many Third World countries today is another symptom of the exploitation and dependency experienced by underdeveloped countries. Repression of civil liberties, removal of democratic freedoms, along with the torture and murder of political prisoners has become a way of life in a growing number of military regimes in the Third World.

Military Regimes

In Asia, Africa and Latin America today, military dictatorships outnumber democratic civilian governments. In Latin America, no less than twenty-two countries are now governed by military regimes. In South East Asia, military regimes exist in Thailand, South Korea, Indonesia, Cambodia and Laos. And, in southern Africa, suppression of the black majority continues under apartheid regimes, along with military governments in Uganda, Ghana and a variety of other African countries. The doctrine of "national security" is used to rationalize the use of armed forces to control civil liberties. According to this doctrine, control of civil liberties is necessary to provide a stable climate for foreign investment and economic growth. Trade union activities are either directly outlawed or strictly controlled. Under these conditions, the poorest sectors of the population are forced to bear the heaviest burden and make the largest sacrifices. Moreover, an increasing number of bishops, priests, and religious who have actively opposed military regimes have themselves become targets of repression.

(A) Brewin, Duclos, MacDonald, **One Gigantic Prison,** Inter-Church Committee on Chile, Toronto, Ontario, 1976, 85 pages.

This is the report of a fact-finding mission to Chile, Argentina and Uruguay in October 1976, by members of the Federal Parliament. Available from the Inter-Church Committee on Human Rights in Latin America, 40 St Clair Avenue East, Suite 201, Toronto, Ontario, M4T 1M9.

(S) Comblin, J., **Le pouvoir militaire en Amérique latine. L'idéologie de la sécurité nationale,** Ed. Jean-Pierre Delarge, Paris, 1977.

Etude sur l'idéologie que les régimes militaires d'Amérique latine ont élaborée pour justifier leur politique intérieure, leur système policier et leur pratique de la torture. Disponible en librairie.

(A) Development and Peace, **A Time to Act,** Toronto, 1978.

A kit of resource materials on the apartheid regime in South Africa and the struggle of black people in South Africa today. Available on order from Development and Peace, 67 Bond Street, Toronto, Ontario.

(S)(A) **Investment in Oppression,** Young Women's Christian Association, 1972, 36 pages.

A study on racial repression in the apartheid regime of South Africa and the impact of foreign investment. Available on order from the Task Force on Churches and Corporate Responsibility, 600 Jarvis Street, Toronto, Ontario.

(S)(A) **Les chrétiens d'Amérique latine: témoins de Jésus-Christ sur un continent devenu une gigantesque prison,** Comité chrétien pour les droits de l'homme en Amérique latine, Montréal, 1978, 67 pages.

Un dossier sur différentes luttes menées par les chrétiens d'Amérique latine. Disponible au Comité chrétien pour les droits de l'homme en Amérique latine, 6558 St-Denis, Montréal, Québec.

(S) Petras, J., **La nouvelle moralité du président Carter et la logique de l'impérialisme,** communication présentée au Congrès sur les droits de l'homme et la conscience chrétienne, organisé par l'Entraide missionnaire Inc., Montréal, Québec, 9-11 septembre 1977.

Ce texte tente de cerner les causes réelles des violations des droits humains. Disponible à Entraide missionnaire Inc., 2295 rue Chambly, Montréal, Québec.

(A) **Somewhere in Asia Human Rights Are Being Trampled Upon,** Canada-Asia Group, Toronto, Ontario, 1978.

An analysis of repression of human rights in Korea and the Phillipines. Available on order from the Canada-Asia Working Group, 11 Madison Avenue, Toronto, Ontario.

(A) **The Universal Declaration of Human Rights,** Inter-Church Committee on Human Rights in Latin America, Toronto, Ontario, 1978.

A guide to the U.N. Declaration on human rights and corresponding social teachings of the Church. Available on order from the Inter-Church Committee on Human Rights in Latin America, c/o 40 St Clair Avenue East, Toronto, Ontario.

Canadian Implications

While most Canadians abhor the presence of military dictatorships, Canada's economic ties serve to support and strengthen military regimes in several countries. Canadian funds, for example, are involved in multi-million dollar loans to the apartheid government of South Africa and the military Junta of Chile. In effect such investment serves to legitimize these repressive regimes and strengthen the hand of oppression in those countries. Furthermore, Canadian-based corporations are known to have taken advantage of controlled trade union conditions, cheap labour, and other investment incentives in Chile, Brazil, Guatamala, Indonesia, and the Dominican Republic. And Canada's Export Development Corporation assists the operations of Canadian companies in several military regimes through loans and other forms of financial assistance.

(A)   **Banking in Apartheid,** Task Force on Churches and Corporate Responsibility, 1977, 4 pages.

A pamphlet outlining the impact of Canadian loans with suggestions for local action. Available on order from the Task Force on Churches and Corporate Responsibility, 600 Jarvis Street, Toronto, Ontario.

(A)   **Letter to the Bank of Montreal,** Canadian Conference of Catholic bishops, 1978, 7 pages.

A statement outlining the position of the Canadian bishops in opposing bank loans to South Africa and Chile. Available at cost on order from the Publication Service, Canadian Conference of Catholic Bishops, 90 Parent Avenue, Ottawa, Ontario, K1N 7B1.

(A)   **Newsletter,** Inter-Church Committee on Human Rights in Latin America, Toronto, Ontario.

A monthly publication which provides case studies of human rights repression in Latin American countries including the relationship of Canadian political and economic policies. Available on order from the Inter-Church Committee on Human Rights in Latin America, 40 St Clair Avenue East, Toronto, Ontario, M4T 1M9.

(A)   **One Body: Human Rights. A Global Struggle,** Issues Nos. 19 and 20, United Church of Canada, Toronto, Ontario, 1978.

A popular analysis of the global struggle for human rights, the role of the Church and the Canadian implications. Available on order from the United Church of Canada, Department of Church and Society, 85 St Clair Avenue East, Toronto, Ontario.

(A)   **Why Chile?** Task Force on Churches and Corporate Responsibility, Toronto, Ontario, 1978, 8 pages.

A pamphlet criticizing Canadian bank loans and proposed investments of Canadian mining companies in support of the military Junta of Chile. Available on order from the Task Force on Churches and Corporate Responsibility, 600 Jarvis Street, Toronto, Ontario

Some Christian Education-Action Programmes

The growing repression of human rights in the Third World (and elsewhere) has become a major focus for the Church in recent years. The Inter-Church Committee on Human Rights in Latin America and its counterpart le Comité chrétien pour les droits de l'homme en Amérique latine have been documenting cases of repression in many Latin American countries. In 1977, for example, these projects sponsored a fact-finding mission by a team of Canadian members of Parliament to Chile, Argentina and Uruguay. More recently, similar fact-finding trips have been undertaken in Nicaragua, Guatemala and El Salvador. The Task Force on Churches and Corporate Responsibility has also launched public education campaigns against continuing Canadian bank loans and foreign investment in South Africa and Chile. In addition, Développement et Paix, the Scarborough Foreign Mission Society and la Société des missions étrangères have made the continuing repression of human rights a major priority in their education and pastoral programmes. Development and Peace, for example, has sponsored a large education programme on the repression of apartheid in southern Africa. And, Amnesty International continues to sponsor letter- writing campaigns in support of political prisoners in military regimes all over the world.

*For further information, contact: Inter-Church Committee on Human Rights in Latin America, c/o 40 St Clair Avenue East, Toronto, Ontario (Tel.: 416-921-4152); Development and Peace, Education Co-ordinator, 67 Bond Street, Toronto, Ontario(Tel.: 416-868-0540); Task Force on Churches and Corporate Responsibility, c/o 600 Jarvis Street, Toronto, Ontario, M4Y 2J6 (Tel.: 416-923-1758); Amnesty International, c/o 2101 Algonquin Avenue, Ottawa, Ontario (Tel.: 613-722-1988).

Some Questions for Animators:

1. What are some specific examples of Third World countries where there is widespread repression of civil and political liberties? Have you or your group had some practical experience in educating and acting on these issues?

2. What research or case studies are useful for analyzing military regimes in the Third World and the causes of repression? The implication of Canadian institutions? What are the conclusions of these studies?

3. What critical insights can be found in the Scriptures and the social teachings of the Church? What specific ethical or theological judgments can be made about these issues?

4. What can be done to develop more critical awareness among people in your community or region? What types of awareness programmes can be developed for education and action on these issues? What methods and tools for animation are most helpful?

5. What kind of organizations are directly engaged in education and action on the repression of human rights in Third World countries? What kind of co-operation or working relationship could be developed with these groups?

6. What relevant connections can made between the repression of civil liberties in various Third World countries and forms of repression that may have occurred from time to time in our own society or region?

7. What forms of action might be taken to change the policies of the Canadian-based corporations operating in Third World countries ruled by military regimes?

9. Military Armament

"In a world of such uneven power, neither justice nor liberation nor co-operation is conceivable, so long as the nations are at one only in their cupidities and their fears, spending 200 billion dollars to defend their so-called security and thirty times less to root out the basic causes of insecurity.
(Maurice Cardinal Roy, President of the Pontifical Commission for Justice and Peace, **Statement on the occasion of the launching of the Second Development Decade,** *1970)*

The international arms race continues to be a scandalous enterprise. For the industrialized powers not only place far greater priority on producing armaments than on eliminating the sufferings of the poor and the oppressed but they have contributed to the military build-up in the Third World.

Military Aid

In 1977, world-wide military expenditures were close to 400 billion dollars, thereby draining huge amounts of capital away from building a world of peace through the development of peoples in poor nations of the world. At the same time, the industrialized countries have contributed to the build-up of military regimes in the Third World through military aid. Press reports frequently cite arms sales to developing countries, most of which are financed by loans or grants from the industrialized countries. Along with military aid and arms shipments, the United States and other industrialized countries have also been involved in conducting military training programmes for various repressive regimes, particularly in Latin America.

(S)(A) Pontifical Commission for Justice and Peace, **Holy See and Disarmament,** Vatican City, 1975.

Outlines the teachings of the Church on the whole issue of disarmament. Available on order from your Catholic bookstore or library.

(S)(A) **Peut-on limiter la course aux productions militaires?,** dossier spécial sur l'armement en général dans le Monde Diplomatique, octobre 1978, pp. 17-21.

Une série d'articles sur la course aux armements et au désarmement. Disponible en bibliothéque.

(E)(A) Rudel, Christian, **Les exportations d'armes,** Dossiers Faim et Développement no 8A, Paris, aôut-septembre 1972.

Un bref dossier sur le commerce des armes. Disponible en bibliothèque.

(S)(A) Stockholm International Peace Research Institute, **The Arms Trade with the Third World,** Penguin Books, Harmondsworth, 1975, 362 pages.

With specific reference to military build-up in the Third World. Available on order from your local bookstore.

Canadian Arms Shipment

The Canadian government has also become more actively engaged in arms sales to Third World countries. Canadian-built aircraft engines, for example, have been sold to such repressive regimes as Brazil, Chile and Iran. In the case of Brazil, which is one of Canada's largest customers for military equipment, the Canadian aircraft is being used for counter-insurgency purposes to control domestic population activities rather than for defense purposes against foreign powers. The sales of Candu nuclear reactors to Argentina and India provide further examples. Arms shipments like these can do little to further the real development of people suffering from poverty and oppression in those countries. While such military sales may be good for Canadian business, they contribute to the continuing underdevelopment of peoples in the Third World.

(S) Regehr, E., **Making a Killing, Canada's Arms Industry,** Toronto, Ontario, McClelland and Stewart, 1975, 135 pages.

A book dealing with the arms industry in Canada. Available on order from your local bookstore.

(A) Thomson, M. and Regehr, E., **A Time to Disarm,** Montréal, Harvest House, 1978, 38 pages.

A discussion guide for stimulating a national dialogue on armament in Canada and in the world. Available from Project Ploughshares, Conrad Grebel College, Waterloo, Ontario, N2L 3G6.

(A) **Ploughshares Monitor,** Project Ploughshares, Waterloo.

The newsletter of Project Ploughshares: a Working Group on Canadian Military Policy. Available on order from Project Ploughshares, Conrad Grebel College, Waterloo, Ontario, N2L 3G6.

Some Christian Education-Action Programmes

Responding to increasing evidence of military build-up in the Third World and elsewhere, the Churches began to actively raise ethical questions about Canada's military expenditures. Development and Peace, in collaboration with Project Ploughshares, has initiated some educational projects on Canadian government policies and the arms industry. Under the sponsorship of the major Canadian Churches, Project Ploughshares has been conducting research on the military defense policies of the Canadian government, the arms industry in Canada, the global arms race in general, the proliferation of nuclear weapons, and the export of arms to Third World countries. At the United Nations Special Session on Disarmament in 1978, Project Ploughshares was actively engaged in urging the Canadian government to take leadership on the critical issues.

*For further information, contact: Project Ploughshares, c/o Conrad Grebel College, Waterloo, Ontario, N2L 3G6; Development and Peace, Education Co-ordinator, 67 Bond Street, Toronto, Ontario (Tel.: 416-868-0540).

Some Questions for Animators:

1. What are some specific examples of military build-up in Third World countries? Have you or your group had any practical experiences in educating and acting on these issues?

2. What research or studies are useful for analyzing the problems and causes of military armament in the Third World? Canada's role? What are the conclusions of these studies?

3. What critical insights can be found in the Scriptures or the social teachings of the Church? What specific ethical or theological themes are helpful for animation?

4. What can be done to develop more critical awareness among people in your community or region on this issue? What types of programmes can be developed for education and action on these issues? What methods and tools for animation are most helpful?

5. What kind of organizations are directly involved in education and action on the problems of military armament? What kind of co-operation or working relationships can be established with these groups?

6. What lessons can be learned for our own country from the military build-up of Third World countries and the use of arms to control the activities of civilians?

7. What forms of action could be taken by Christian groups in your community to change the policies of the Canadian government and the arms industry concerning the shipment of armaments to military regimes in Third World countries.

10. Immigration

"...Immigration to Canada is largely caused by the persistence of poverty, underdevelopment, and oppression elsewhere in the world. Refugees flee from oppression and danger. Immigrants come to escape conditions of poverty and exploitation in search of their fair share of opportunities and wealth...

Immigration law reform will not really touch these problems. What is required is the creation of a new social order in Canada and the world, based on a redistribution of wealth and power for the sake of justice and peace."
(*Canadian Bishops,* **Brief to the Joint Parliamentary Committee on Immigration Policy,** *1975)*

To the landless, the hungry, the insecure, and the threatened, the more affluent, industrialized countries seem to offer hope for new opportunities in life. The industrialized countries however, have not been so willing to open their doors and share their resources with people most in need in the Third World.

Selective Immigration

Historically, the immigration policies of industrialized countries have been closely linked with the economic growth of their countries. Economic criteria rather than humanitarian sentiment dominate policies on immigration. Through the use of point systems, the industrialized countries have been able to select immigrants on their own terms. In times of economic growth, the industrialized countries have opened their doors to migrants from poorer countries as sources of cheap labour for industries. More recently, the industrialized countries' immigration policies have favoured skilled labour which has often resulted in a "brain drain" on poor countries. In times of economic recession, immigration policies have generally become very restrictive, closing the door to the entry of people from poor countries. Today, the industrialized world is going through an economic recession which has resulted in restrictive immigration practices.

(S)   Daly, B., **Immigration Policy: It's Impact on Canadian Society,** Toronto, Canadian Council of Christians and Jews, 1978.

A discussion of the economic and racial factors in Canada's immigration policy. Reprinted in K. MacLeod, **Multiculturalism and Bilingualism in an Institutional Setting,** Toronto, Ontario.

(S)   **The Politics of People,** Issue No. 9, United Church of Canada Publication, Toronto, 1975, 8 pages.

Includes an analysis of immigration in the context of the global economy. Available on order from the United Church of Canada, 85 St Clair Avenue East, Toronto, Ontario.

Canadian Immigration

Canada's new immigration law has placed a ceiling on the number of people allowed into the country each year. The point system is largely designed to select people in the prime of their life, who are most adaptable to the Canadian labour force, and who will put the least amount of strain on government social services. By placing heavy emphasis on Canada's economic interests, little concern is given to the importance of sharing the riches of this land with those people who have a vital need for a new homeland. Until recently, very few of Canada's immigration posts were located in Asia, Africa and Latin America. Moreover, Canada has also been inconsistent in responding to the needs of refugees fleeing from repressive political regimes. While Canadian officials have readily responded to political upheavals in Hungary, Czechoslovakia and Uganda by accepting large numbers of refugees, it took a great deal of public pressure before the Canadian government would accept refugees from Chile after the coup in 1973. Indeed, Canadian officials have been reluctant to respond to calls for help from victims of military regimes in Latin America generally. Without a just refugee policy, selections are likely to be made on the basis of political ideology rather than real human needs.

(S) **Working Paper for the Great Canadian Debate about Population and Immigration,** Inter-Church Project on Population, Ottawa, 1975, 34 pages.

A critique of the government's Green Paper on immigration. Available from ICPOP, 90 Parent Avenue, Ottawa, Ontario, K1N 7B1.

(S) **Immigration (Proposed Changes in the Immigration Bill),** Inter-Church Project on Population and the Inter-Church Committee on Human Rights in Latin America, 1978.

A critical analysis of the Immigration Bill by several inter-church projects. While somewhat outdated, the basic points made here are still relevant. Available from ICPOP, 90 Parent Avenue, Ottawa, Ontario, K1N 7B1.

(E) La Ligue des droits de l'homme, **Mémoire sur le Bill C-24 sur l'immigration,** présenté au comité permanent sur le travail, la main-d'oeuvre et l'immigration, 7 juin 1977.

Un regard critique sur le Bill C-24. Disponible à la Ligue des droits de l'homme, 3836 Saint-Hubert, Montréal, Québec, H2L 4A5.

(A) The Canadian bishops have published two pastoral messages on immigration: Social Affairs Commission, **A Pastoral Message on Immigration,** 1975; Commission on Migrants and Tourism, **Strangers in Our Midst,** 1978. Available at cost on order from the Canadian Conference of Catholic Bishops, Publication Service, 90 Parent Avenue, Ottawa, Ontario, K1N 7B1.

Some Christian Education-Action Programmes

In responding to the Canadian government's Green Paper on immigration in 1975, Church groups across the country became involved in raising ethical issues about Canada's population and immigration policies. The Inter-Church Project on Population co-ordinated the research, documentation, and the various activities of Christian groups. Presentations were made to the Joint Parliamentary Committee on Immigration, advocating a variety of proposals for an immigration policy based on social and economic justice. At the same time, Christian groups have been pressing the Canadian government to accept political refugees from Chile, Argentina and other repressive regimes. The Inter-Church Committee on Human Rights in Latin America has played a major role in urging the Canadian government to accept political refugees fleeing from repressive regimes in Latin America, assisting refugees and their families in their relocation and calling on the government to adopt a more just and consistent refugee policy.

*For more information, contact: Inter-Church Project on Population, c/o 90 Parent Avenue, Ottawa, K1N 7B1 (Tel.: 613-236-9461, ext. 265); Inter-Church Committee on Human Rights in Latin America, c/o 40 St Clair Avenue East, Toronto, Ontario (Tel.: 416-921-4152).

Some Questions for Animators:

1. What are some specific problems experienced by immigrants and/or refugees coming from Third World countries? Have you or your group had some practical experience in educating and acting on these issues?

2. What research or studies are useful in analyzing the immigration and refugee policies of industrialized countries? Canada's policies? What are the conclusions of these studies?

3. What critical insights can be found in the Scriptures and the social teachings of the Church? What specific ethical or theological themes are helpful for animation?

4. What can be done to develop more critical awareness among people in your community or region on the issue of Third World immigration? What types of programmes can be initiated for education and action on these issues? What methods and tools for animation are most helpful?

5. What kind of organizations are directly involved in education and action on the issues of immigration and refugees here in Canada? What kind of co-operation or working relationships can be developed with these groups?

6. What relevant connections can be made between the dynamics of immigration from Third World countries and the dynamics of migration between hinterland and metropolitan centers in our own society or region?

7. What forms of action could be taken by Christian groups in your community to change the restrictive aspects of Canadian immigration and refugee policies?

Table of Contents

Photo Credits

If through inadvertence, any photo has been printed without permission, proper acknowledgement will be made in future printings after notice has been received.

Cover Page:

Photos appearing on the cover are identified clock-wise commencing from left hand corner.

Photos-Service "vivant univers"
"Exodus" etching by Ed Bartram;
    photograph by Thomas E. Moore (© C.C.C. 1976)
Photos-Service "vivante Afrique"
Unknown

Text:

Photos appearing in the text can be identified from left to right as:
(a), (b) or (c)

The Catholic Register: p. 9(a); p. 14(c)
Ellefsen Photographe Ltée.: p. 4(b); p. 4(c); p. 72(b); p. 72(c).
Gilles Lafrance: p. 72(a).
Kevin Moynahan Audio-Visual Services: p. 9(b); p. 14(b); p. 35(a), (b), (c);
                                             p. 46(c); p. 60(a).
National Film Board of Canada-Phototeque:
                         p. 19(a) by George Hunter; p. 46(a);
                         p. 46(B) by Jack Long; p. 60(b); p. 60(c); p. 105(a)
Bill Paul: p. 111(b)
Photos-Service "vivante Afrique": p. 89(a); p. 105(b)
Photos-Service "vivant univers": p. 14(a); p. 89 (b); p. 89(c); p. 96(a); p. 96(c).
Religious News Service Photo: p. 111(c); p. 9(c) by Susan McKinney.
H. Armstrong Robertson: p. 19(b).
Unknown: p. 96(b); p. 105(c); p. 111(a).
Jean-Marie Versteege: p. 4(a); p. 19(c).